Ordinary People and the Media

The Demotic Turn

Graeme Turner

SAGE

Los Angeles | London | New Delhi
Singapore | Washington DC

© Graeme Turner 2010

First published 2010

Published in association with Theory, Culture & Society, Nottingham Trent University.

SAGE Publications Ltd
1 Oliver's Yard
55 City Road
London EC1Y 1SP

SAGE Publications Inc.
2455 Teller Road
Thousand Oaks, California 91320

SAGE Publications India Pvt Ltd
B 1/I 1 Mohan Cooperative Industrial Area
Mathura Road, Post Bag 7
New Delhi 110 044

SAGE Publications Asia-Pacific Pte Ltd
33 Pekin Street #02-01
Far East Square
Singapore 048763

Library of Congress Control Number: 2009924990

British Library Cataloguing in Publication data

A catalogue record for this book is available from the British Library

ISBN 978-1-84860-166-6
ISBN 978-1-84860-167-3 (pbk)

Typeset by C&M Digitals (P) Ltd, Chennai, India
Printed in India at Replika Press Pvt Ltd
Printed on paper from sustainable resources

Contents

Graeme Turner takes a balanced and exceptionally reasonable approach to assessing the strengths and weaknesses of the demotic turn in cultural studies.

Jim McGuigan, Professor of Cultural Analysis and Sociology, Loughborough University

Turner's book examines rigorously perhaps the most important debate within TV Studies; the relationships between the medium and the ordinary people who appear on it and consume it. Using a wealth of international examples, Turner explores diverse ideas such as new media, community radio and reality TV to show how all forms of media can be understood within the rubric of the ordinary. Smartly and engagingly written, this book draws on Turner's extensive work in this area to show how thinking about ordinary people and media offers valuable insights into areas such as globalisation, media industries, participation, representation, cultural politics and technology.

Brett Mills, Lecturer in Film and Television Studies, University of East Anglia

Graeme Turner provides an outstanding intervention in contemporary debates about the emancipatory potential of the new media landscape. While "power to the people" may be the rallying cry in an age of blogging, Web 2.0 interactivity, and reality TV, Turner cautions against confusing the "demotic" with democracy. His deft analysis of how the media industries profit from the promotion of individualism and the "ordinary" compels us to revisit fundamental questions of power, identity, and community. *Ordinary People and the Media* is required reading for students and scholars navigating the shifting terrain of media and cultural studies.

Serra Tinic, Associate Professor of Theory and Culture, University of Alberta

Graeme Turner is one of the most interesting and thoughtful writers in the field of media and cultural studies. Ordinary People and the Demotic Turn is a book full of perceptive ideas and critical insights. Starting from the recognition that there has never been a time when so many ordinary people have been so visible in the media, Turner explores what this means for ordinary people, the media, and media and cultural analysis. This is a wonderful book that should be read by all serious students of contemporary media and culture.

John Storey, Director of the Centre for Research in Media and Cultural Studies, University of Sunderland

Acknowledgements

Here, I would like to acknowledge some of those who have played a part in helping to bring this book together. First and foremost is my editor at Sage, Chris Rojek, who has not only taken this on as a publishing project but has also contributed significantly to the thought which has gone into it, and whose conversations over the last five or six years have proved highly stimulating provocations to my thinking through these issues. I would also like to thank the editors of the *Theory, Culture & Society* series for their support for this project; it is indeed a privilege to be published within this distinguished set of books.

Thanks, also, to a wonderful group of colleagues at the Centre for Critical and Cultural Studies (CCCS) at the University of Queensland who have listened to the ideas in this book for some time now, in work-in-progress sessions and personal conversations; who have made helpful and informed suggestions about how best to prosecute them; and who, most importantly, have provided me with the most stimulating and collegial work environment an academic could desire.

Two CCCS colleagues in particular, Mark Andrejevic and Melissa Gregg, with whom I had the pleasure of co-teaching a graduate class on media consumption in 2008, have generously given up their time to look at draft material and make helpful and thoughtful comments. Jean Burgess and Jason Wilson also looked at drafts of sections of the book and provided me with generous and useful comments and suggestions.

John Hartley may disagree with much of what is written in this book and therefore may not really want my thanks, but he nevertheless remains, as both friend and colleague, a most valued and robust interlocutor on all things to do with the media and culture. Toby Miller, too, has been someone with whom conversations about the planning, structure and orientation of this project have been especially valuable over the last couple of years.

I would also like to thank the editors of two journals for their permission to incorporate revised and expanded versions of published material in Chapters 1 and 4. The material concerned was originally published as 'The mass production of celebrity: celetoids, reality TV and the "demotic turn"' in 2006 in the *International Journal of Cultural Studies* (9(2)), and as 'Politics, radio and journalism in Australia: the influence of "talkback"', in 2009 in *Journalism: Theory, Practice, and Criticism* (10(4)).

Finally, I wish to gratefully acknowledge the contribution made to this project by the funding provided through my Australian Research Council Federation Fellowship; being able to work solely on research as a result of this fellowship is truly a rare and wonderful opportunity.

Introduction: the demotic turn

[**demotic** (adjective): 'of or for the common people']

It has become commonplace to notice the increasing number of opportunities for ordinary people to appear in the media. From the *vox pops* in news bulletins to the celebrity that comes with participation in reality TV, from calling up your local talk radio host to competing for stardom in *Idol*, from posting your favourite images on Facebook to becoming one of the notorious Web 'cam-girls' – the possibilities of media visibility seem endless. The causes are many: the pervasiveness of celebrity, shifts in television from drama to 'live' formats, and the interactivity of Web 2.0, among them. The ordinary citizen's access to a media profile that was unavailable before the digital revolution has encouraged some to argue that we have entered an unprecedented era of networked information, which in turn provides opportunities for participation that are so widespread and various that they constitute a form of democratization – an opening up of the media on a scale that invites us to think of it as a new form of political enfranchisement.

At the same time, the character of much of this access and some of its results must compromise this possibility. The 'cam-girls' web-sites, I have suggested elsewhere (Turner, 2004), are only one click away from porn sites; the proliferation of blogs is not solely driven by progressive or liberal political attitudes – it houses political extremism just as comfortably; the media's interest in their reality and game show contestants is at least as exploitative as it is enabling; and the rise in the political influence of talk radio in the USA, Europe and Australia has been marked by the divisive, and commercial, deployment of that power rather than by its building of broad-based consensus. One can't jump to the conclusion that a widening of access necessarily carries with it a democratic politics.

Furthermore, the strategies through which the media industries have developed popular access to their programming formats are themselves worth examining. This is an age in which the media have been especially active in constructing celebrity, and other forms of identity as well, as the available means to a commercial end. At the same time, the consumption of media has become so individualized and fragmented that the notion that the media should bear some kind of social or community responsibility seems, to many, anachronistic. Paradoxically, expectations that the media might serve the public good seem to have been displaced at the very same time when media performances by members of the public have never been more visible. The function of the media, for so long connected to assumptions about the role of the fourth estate, about its implication in the construction of the citizen, and about the importance of the provision of information to the public as a means of enabling the proper functioning of the democratic state, now looks as if it must be explained in relation to a range of other, quite different, assumptions.

In *Understanding Celebrity* (2004), I challenged the democratic implications so frequently read into the politics of media access in contemporary cultural and media studies. In doing this, I was following a line of thought that had occupied me for some years, but which had been initiated by a comment made by a colleague, Liz Jacka, in response to an earlier discussion which had taken for granted a connection between ordinary people's representation in the media and a process of democratization. Jacka insisted, and I think rightly, that this was a step too far: that while there was certainly clear evidence of an increased demotic access to the media, one needed more evidence of the actual politics involved in each instance before one was entitled to assume that it served democratic purposes. In *Understanding Celebrity*, I coined the term 'the demotic turn' as a preferred means of referring to the increasing visibility of the 'ordinary person' as they have turned themselves into media content through celebrity culture, reality TV, DIY web-sites, talk radio and the like. In the context of that book, it was used as a means of understanding the proliferation of celebrity across the media since the 1980s, as well as celebrity's colonization of the expectations of everyday life in contemporary western societies, particularly among teenagers and young adults. Where there was a crossover between certain aspects of reality TV and the production of celebrity, I was concerned to argue for the importance of recognizing how identity was being constituted in such formats. Even though the contestants on *Idol* may be competing for the chance to become a successful singer, we frequently find them arguing their case to the judges in terms of their essential selves – their intrinsic star quality – rather than in terms of their musical skills or abilities. Much of the participation in reality TV, then, is aimed at a certain kind of recognition of the self.

This book is aimed at further developing and applying the idea of the 'demotic turn', not only because of its implication in the construction of celebrity but also, more importantly, because of its implication in what I regard as a new field of relations opening up between media and culture. The media, and in particular television, have developed new capacities for constructing identities and these capacities are producing social effects that are about more than just the production of *Big Brother*. Indeed, I want to argue that the function of the media has mutated as it has participated, increasingly directly, in the construction of cultural identity as one of its primary spheres of activity. As I have put it elsewhere (Turner, 2006), where the media might once have operated as a mediator or perhaps a broadcaster of cultural identities, its contemporary function is closer to that of a translator or even an author of identities.

I acknowledge that some of this book will be critical of the politics of participation it examines: it does seem to me, for example, that there are instances where it would be appropriate if the activity of certain populist talk radio hosts was recognized as constituting an abuse of media power rather than an instance of the robust operation of a democratic public sphere. More generally, however, the book's primary, and broader, objective is to examine closely what is going on in these new media developments, and what kinds of potentials they actually offer to the ordinary people involved. Since so much industry and academic discussion has been focused upon an optimistic reading of these developments which highlights their democratizing potential, and since my interest is precisely in testing and qualifying the claims made for them, I am involved in an inescapably critical project. That still seems to me a fundamental objective for a cultural studies analysis of the media – as Charlotte

Brunsdon has put it in another context, of a cultural criticism which is 'attentive to, but not seduced by', current conditions (2009: 30).

What follows, then, is *not* just another anti-tabloidization argument, an account of the media's 'dumbing down', or a contribution to the venerable tradition of moralizing critiques of popular media (Hartley, 2009: 18) that made cultural studies necessary in the first place. Rather, my objective is to ask if there has been a structural shift in what the media are doing, some (not all) of the time, and if the explosion of celebrity, reality TV, and user-generated content on the Web and so on, that has generated this new visibility of ordinary people in the media as performers and producers actually reflects something more fundamental than contemporary media fashion. If it does, then that would be worth knowing.

There has been much debate about the topics taken up in this book. As we will see in the following chapters, there are strongly contrasting views on what we should make of, for instance, the cultural effects of reality TV, the pervasiveness of celebrity, and the populism of the radio shock-jocks. There are also vigorous debates about exactly how much influence ordinary people actually exert as they increase their participation in the media. Depending on who you read, for instance, 'citizen journalism' can be the saviour of the democratic fourth estate or a failed utopian dream; downloading video online can be the future of television or an overblown sideshow; user-generated content on the internet can be *the* core activity for the next generation of media industries or merely the plaything of self-promoting early adopters. The changes I am examining have been variously described as top-down, bottom-up, and a combination of both.

This is particularly the case in relation to the more participatory and interactive media formats such as reality TV and the various capacities of Web 2.0. In these cases, especially, the diversity of competing positions seems matched by the intensity with which each is argued. To take a clear position on any of this material – and I would have to say particularly one that is sceptical about the discourse of emancipation, democratization and liberation that has become the default position for so many media and cultural studies' accounts of Web 2.0 lately – is to enter into a very testy debate. And yet, despite the competing certainties which abound, the issues are deeply complicated and their playing out in any specific instance fundamentally contingent. Furthermore, in a context where change is rapid and where only limited verifiable independent research is available, there is a problem of proportion; that is, while there is at least an element of truth in most of what is being said, the excessive claims that are characteristically made on behalf of each new technological development clearly test some readers' credulity and patience:

> The focus is on micro-events of insignificance that are puffed into an historical revelation of biblical importance. Bookshelves are filled with tipping points and wisdom of crowds. Chris Anderson's *The Long Tail* captures an argument so simple it can be conveyed through the title. He investigated Amazon, eBay and online music retailers to show how 'endless choice' is creating 'unlimited demand'. He argues that the focus on best-sellers is misguided and the internet has changed 'everything'. Technological determinism is fused with neoliberalism, where the market promises endless growth and choice. (Brabazon, 2008: 16)

A further consideration is that many of the arguments made about ordinary people's access to the media, and to the cultural, creative and participatory opportunities this provides, are made by those who are far from 'ordinary' themselves: cultural, political, academic and media elites, sometimes personally or professionally identified with the media programme or capacity they are boosting. Often, as I will argue throughout the following chapters, what these arguments need most of all is a reality check that can run against the influence of activist advocacy, geeky enthusiasm and industry spin.

The topics dealt with in this book include the rise of celebrity, reality TV, news and current affairs journalism on- and offline, citizen journalism, talk radio, blogging and user-generated content online. The participation of ordinary people is fundamental to all of these media activities. As we go through the book, however, it becomes clear that while the participation of ordinary people is continually claimed as the benefit to be realized from each new development, their actual participation becomes less and less the focus of investigation and research – indeed simply less of an explicit issue – in the relevant academic debates. So while the role of ordinary people in reality TV (dealt with in Chapters 1 and 2) is a central debate in discussions of this format – and there are many views on what needs to be said about that – the role of ordinary people in discussions of user-generated content online (see Chapter 5) is almost entirely notional. That is, while their participation is hailed as a fundamental attribute of the uses of these technologies, there is almost nothing written about, and very little empirical research[1] which examines, what use 'actual' ordinary people might make of them, and how they might reap the benefits assumed to flow from their access.[2]

That is a lot to leave out, because there are so many different kinds of ordinary people we need to consider: those who are cast to appear on reality TV, those who get to talk to radio hosts on air, those who contribute their comments to blogs online, those who use YouTube to watch their favourite DIY video, or those who use their MySpace page to broadcast their identities around the world. And, then, of course, there are the many, many more, who participate by just watching, reading or listening.

In this book, I use the demotic turn as a means of examining what I argue is a significant new development in how the media participate in the production of culture. The examples discussed will be drawn from an international range of locations and research. In Chapter 1 (*Ordinary People: celebrity, tabloid culture and the function of the media*), I outline the central argument of this volume. While the idea of the demotic turn emerges as a way of describing the increased participation of ordinary people in the media, it has a more widespread potential for helping us to better understand the cultural function of a commercial media system that is more focused on the distribution of entertainment and the production of cultural identities than ever before. The chapter differentiates the approach taken in this book from familiar taste-based critiques of the media, such as those most commonly identified with the notion of tabloidization. While the concept of tabloidization is implicated here – in many ways, the demotic turn is an alternative, less perjorative and more productive, way of understanding some of the shifts in content and participation often noticed in critiques of the tabloid – the focus is not primarily on the content of media texts or the taste-based cultures within which they might be marketed. Rather, the long history of discussions of the 'tabloid' alerts us to some of the territories we might examine for the signs of a fundamental shift in the media's cultural function.

Chapter 2 deals with reality TV and the construction of cultural identities. Earlier, I suggested that the media no longer operate as merely the mediators of cultural identities but now serve the function of a translator or author of cultural identities. Reality TV in its various guises has been a key site for the examination of this issue, and for debates about the various kinds of cultural influences such programming formats, and the particular way in which they have been performed in recent years, may well have on the cultures which consume them. The success of transnational hybrid formats such as *Big Brother* and *Idol* has introduced new, and more urgent, dimensions to what had become relatively familiar debates about the globalization, 'glocalization' or homogenization of culture. The fact these formats claim to provide us with unmediated presentations of 'everyday' life has generated concern about their influence over how they ask us, implicitly, to think about our lives, about the norms which govern them and the possibilities they offer.

These concerns have been especially urgent in non-western developed nations where these formats have built large audiences and where, as we shall see in Chapter 2, there is often a massive demand from prospective participants. The gap between the cultural systems embedded in the television format, no matter how 'localized' or 'indigenized' it has become, and the cultural systems of the nation-state in which it is broadcast, is often profound – raising new questions about the role that television plays in constructing culture. This chapter will examine these issues as they have been dealt with in western television studies, before then going on to discuss significant examples from the East Asian region and the Middle East, where the conflict between the identities constructed through television and those constructed through the nation-state has been explicitly addressed by both government and the public.

Chapter 3 (*Redefining Journalism: citizens, blogs and the rise of opinion*) addresses a number of the key concerns in what has become a serious transnational debate about the future of the western, fourth estate, version of journalism. As the traditional print media lose much of their readership, and as news and current affairs on radio and television lose much of their audience in many locations, the opportunities provided by developments online have attracted increasing attention. Public journalism projects, citizen journalism ventures, and the political blog have all been nominated by various analysts as providing the direction for a future in which the disappearance of traditional journalism is regarded as more or less inevitable.

The context for these developments is not only that of a commercial crisis for the large news industries. These industries are also facing a crisis of credibility and authority: the perception that the mainstream news media have lost their connection to the community, and that they are no longer sufficiently reliable as an independent source of information and analysis. The work of the amateur or pro-am reporter and the opinions of the blogger have gained an audience because of what is seen to be their connection to ordinary people – that is, their demotic dimension. In many of these locations, however, the presentation of news has merged with the presentation of opinion and there is little interest in policing the boundaries between them by restoring the editorial function. Indeed, there is a sense that the open declaration of opinion is in many ways a more honest, reliable and acceptable tactic than what had come to be seen as a spurious performance of objectivity. The attraction of opinion, rather than verifiable information, is reflected in the increasing numbers using political blogs as news sources, as well as participating through posting comments and engaging in conversations with those others who also choose to participate in this way. This trend has affected the approach taken by the mainstream news media as well as how they now look for ways to turn news into entertainment; in particular, the US TV network FOX has achieved commercial success by presenting highly opinionated news and current affairs.

The highwater mark for opinionated news and current affairs, however, can be found in the populist formations of talk radio that dominate the airwaves in (at least) the USA, Australia and some parts of Europe. The development of talk radio in the United States and Australia has seen radio news and current affairs turned over to the audience, moderated by a host who is responsible for making the programme entertaining. The caller's voice supplies the programme with its demotic authenticity, and the host with his (and it is usually his) legitimacy. Chapter 4

(*Talk Radio, Populism and the Demotic Voice*) examines several case studies: the role of 'talkback' radio in Australia in what came to be called the Cronulla riots (so-called 'race riots' in Sydney in 2005) and the populist talk radio host Rush Limbaugh in the USA. While the rationale for talk radio has been explicitly egalitarian – the Australian example is talked of as 'God's great leveller' – it is notable that what has happened in practice has often been far from liberal or tolerant. American talk radio is dominated by deeply conservative political voices and the Australian example has been accused of directly inflaming the racial tensions that resulted in the Cronulla riots. The participation of the public in these programmes is fundamental to the format, and yet the diversity and tolerance one might expect to flow from such participation are definitely not markers of the format's performance in practice. Indeed, the commercial point of the programmes seems to be to employ populist politics as a means of specifying its audience, even if that results in sharpening political divisions within the wider listening public. At the end of this chapter, the distinction between populism and the demotic is examined, before debates about populism and cultural studies – debates first held in the early 1990s – are reprised.

The point of reviewing these debates is to contextualize the way that cultural and media studies have tended to deal with the political potentials of Web 2.0 and, in particular, user-generated content online. Chapter 5 (*Revenge of the Nerds: user-generated content online*) acknowledges the fact that DIY celebrities, social networking sites, blogging and DIY video online have altered the balance of power between the producer and the consumer in ways that repay close examination. Those who would argue that user-generated content is the clearest sign of the reclamation of consumer sovereignty within the mediascape certainly have plenty of arresting evidence to draw upon – even if it is geographically concentrated in the affluent West. However, the chapter also notes the exorbitance and indeed the self-interestedness of some of the claims that have been made for the cultural and political benefits of the digital revolution. There are clear areas of exaggeration in the standard accounts of digital media which emerge from the industry and the academy to do with the scale of the shift to the 'produser', for instance, or the challenge posed to traditional media such as television by online video. There is also the undeniable fact that these arguments are products of a western media elite: white, male, early adopters, probably residing in the USA, are presenting arguments for which they claim a global provenance. On the other hand, the scale of the international take-up of social networking suggests that there are genuinely new functions for the media under development which would repay research and closer analysis. This chapter, then, examines these issues in relation to user-generated content online – blogging, DIY videos on YouTube and social networking.

It has become commonplace to describe the current mediascape as constituting the infrastructure for an 'information society'. In my concluding chapter (*The Entertainment Age: the media and consumption today*) I suggest that the overwhelming global trend towards the commercialization of the media as entertainment industries encourages an alternative formulation – that we are now entering an age in which entertainment has become increasingly important. In light of that context, this chapter sets out to understand what kinds of functions the media now serve politically and culturally as they divest themselves of the responsibilities of being providers of information to their citizenry; as they increasingly see themselves as commercial entities responsible to their shareholders rather than the community or nation; as they find new ways to incorporate user-generated content into their menus of entertainment; and as they increasingly invest in the production of social identities as a means of pump-priming the market for other products. These shifts in the media's idea of themselves have not reduced their social, political and cultural centrality. Indeed, as I have outlined in the preceding chapters, in some ways this has taken on an even more active cultural role. That cultural role, however, is largely driven by the media's commercial interests and thinking about what this might mean is the focus of the final chapter.

Notes

1 Indeed, in one case, an academic blogger in Australia made an extraordinary argument, within a highly defensive review of a book

critical of the claims of 'digital democracy', which implied that the Web is so dynamic, and research materials so 'static', that there is virtually no point in subjecting the Web to academic research (Bahnisch, 2009)!

2 An interesting exception to this that I am not going to have space to deal with here, is the programme of research projects connected to the digital storytelling movement, interventions at the community level which clearly do focus on the development of the participatory media skills of 'actual' ordinary people (see Hartley and McWilliam, 2009a; McWilliam, 2009; Tacchi, 2009).

1

Ordinary People: celebrity, tabloid culture, and the function of the media[1]

Ordinary celebrities

Let me begin by reviewing the recent trends in the production of celebrity which provoke the kind of questions I want to raise. I am by no means the first to have noticed what has become quite a programmatic shift in the preferred territory for the development of celebrity through particular media platforms – television and the internet in particular. This is a shift from the elite to the ordinary. 'Ordinariness', to be sure, has always occupied a place among the repertoire of celebrity discourses as well as within the core programming formats of western television itself (Bonner, 2003). Elsewhere, Frances Bonner, P. David Marshall and I have pointed out the contradictoriness of the discourses of celebrity – their capacity to simultaneously valorize a celebrity's elite status while nonetheless celebrating their 'intrinsic ordinariness' (Turner et al., 2000: 13). It is also true that 'ordinary people' have always been 'discovered', suddenly extracted from their everyday lives and processed for stardom; both the film and the music industry incorporated such processes into their cultural mythologies as well as their industrial practice many years ago. In recent times, however, the use of this practice has grown dramatically and become far more systematic. Whole media formats are now devoted to it, and the contemporary media consumer has become increasingly accustomed to following what happens to the 'ordinary' person who has been plucked from obscurity to enjoy a highly circumscribed celebrity. The *Big Brother* housemates are the most obvious example[2] and, among these, it has turned out, 'ordinariness' is so fundamental to their casting that it is non-negotiable. In some local versions of the format, *Big Brother* housemates have been evicted after they were found to be already working within the entertainment industry and thus attempting to merge their new visibility as celebritized 'ordinary people' with a pre-existing media career.

The trend has a broader provenance than the casting of *Big Brother*, however. As Nick Couldry points out, ordinary people have never been more desired by, or more visible within, the media; nor have their own utterances ever been reproduced with the faithfulness, respect and accuracy that they are today (Couldry, 2003: 102).

The explosion of reality TV, confessional talk formats, docusoaps and so-called reality-based game shows over the last decade has significantly enhanced television's demand for ordinary people desiring 'celebrification'. The expansion of both the demand and the supply side has occurred in a symbiotic and accelerating cycle fuelled by the relatively sudden expansion of the global trade in TV formats. Although the 'reality' of reality TV is of course a construction, what has become significant is the way these formats have exploited the reality effect of television's 'liveness': namely, the foregrounded liveness (as in, what we are watching is happening right now!) enhances the illusion that what is being watched is real or genuine, thus challenging the competing suspicion that it is only being staged for the camera. Indeed, reality TV is often quite exorbitantly 'live': it is occurring in real time as we watch it on a live video-stream via the internet, and those wishing to interact with it directly can do so by accessing one of the web-sites or online chatrooms, or by participating in the audience vote. Stripped across the schedule for months at a time in a set daily timeslot, as it is in many countries, *Big Brother* is not only received as a live media event, it also becomes embedded in the routine daily structures of the audience's everyday lives. (It may well be *that* which is the most significant 'reality' effect of reality TV, not what is actually happening in the house or on the *Idol* audition set.)

Among the consequences of this trend towards developing the ordinary celebrity through the success of reality TV formats is an acceleration of the industrial cycle of use and disposal for the products of such programmes. If performing on *Big Brother* can generate celebrity within a matter of days, this same celebrity can also disappear just as quickly. In fact, it is essential that each crop of *Big Brother* housemates can be easily replaced by the next group if the format is to successfully reproduce itself, series after series. In this regard, television's production of celebrity can truly be regarded as a manufacturing process into which the product's planned obsolescence is incorporated. And that product is manufactured for a particular audience. The replaceable celebrity-commodity (Turner et al., 2000: 12–13) is structurally fundamental to both of the leading primetime formats aimed at the key 14–35-year-old demographics in most western markets: reality TV and soap opera. In order to define this particular iteration of celebrity – the individual with no particular talents that might encourage expectations of work in the entertainment industry, no specific career objectives beyond the achievement of media visibility, and an especially short lifecycle as a public figure – Chris Rojek has coined the term 'celetoid':

> Celetoids are the accessories of cultures organized around mass communications and staged authenticity. Examples include lottery winners, one-hit wonders, stalkers, whistle-blowers, sports' arena streakers, have-a-go-heroes, mistresses of public figures and the various other social types who command media attention one day, and are forgotten the next. (2001: 20–1)

Given what appears to be our culture's appetite for consuming celebrity and the scale of demand for the new stories, gossip and pictures the celebrity media industries generate,[3] the accelerated commodity lifecycle of the celetoid has emerged as an effective industrial solution to the problem of satisfying that demand.

In relation to the broader culture within which the consumption of celebrity occurs, these trends have resulted in the idea of celebrity itself mutating: no longer a magical condition, research suggests that it is fast becoming an almost reasonable expectation for us to have of our everyday lives.[4] The opportunity of becoming a celebrity has spread beyond the various elites and entered into the expectations of the population in general. Among the effects of this, in turn, is the proliferation of various kinds of DIY celebrity; on the internet, in particular, 'celebrification' has become a familiar mode of cyber-self-presentation. As I have discussed in *Understanding Celebrity* (Turner, 2004: Chapter 5), this is sometimes regarded as a reason for optimism, a sign of the egalitarianization of celebrity as the means of production are seized by the ordinary citizen.

The more important development, in my view, is the scale upon which the media have begun to produce celebrity *on their own*. Where once the media were more or less content to pick up celebrities produced through a range of sports, news and entertainment contexts, or to respond to approaches from publicists, promotions and public relations personnel, contemporary television in particular has introduced a much greater degree of vertical integration into the industrial structure which produces their celebrities. In addition to exploiting those who have already been established through other means, television has learnt that it can also invent, produce, market and sell on its celebrities from scratch – and on a much larger scale than ever before. Casting ordinary people into game shows, docu-soaps and reality TV programming enables television producers to 'grow their own' celebrities and to control how they are marketed before, during and after production – all of this while still subordinating the achieved celebrity of each individual to the needs of the particular programme or format. The extent to which this is now done, and the pervasive presence its most successful products can establish, make this an extremely significant shift not only in terms of the production and consumption of celebrity but also in terms of how the media now participate in the cultural construction of identity and desire.

Cultural and media studies have responded in a number of ways to these developments. We have had discussions which helpfully problematize the 'reality' of reality TV, as well as examining the performativeness of the identities on offer through this newly vertically integrated mediascape (that is, the motivated performance of ordinariness or authenticity is the focus of critical analysis and attention: see Kilborn, 2003). There are post-Habermasian critiques which see the mass production of celebrity as yet another instance of the media's tendency to produce simulations of the real as spectacles for consumption, and thus as another instance of the diminution of the public sphere. There are also suggestions, as I noted earlier, that the increased diversity evident in the contemporary production and consumption of celebrity contains a political potential that may well be positive (Dovey, 2000). Among the latter formulations is the argument that such programming engages in particularly direct and useful ways with the socio-cultural process of modelling ethical behaviours and identities (Hay and Ouellette, 2008; Lumby, 2003).

The most influential example in this context, and one upon which I want to build, has been developed through John Hartley's deployment of the term 'democratainment' (1999: see Chapter 12). Hartley has argued in several of his books that we are witnessing the democratization of the media: breaking with more elite formations of popular entertainment, dispensing with the privileging of information and education, and allowing the media to focus on the construction of cultural identities. In *Understanding Celebrity*, I challenged the idea of 'democratainment' by querying the connection it argues between democracy and the proliferation of DIY celebrity, the opening up of media access, and the explosion of 'the ordinary' in media content. I agree with John Hartley that the trends we have both noticed have, among other things, opened up media access to women, to people of colour, and to a wider array of class positions; that the increased volume of media content now available could result in increased powers of self-determination becoming available to media consumers; and that there is every reason why the positive by-products of this increased volume and diversity might excite optimism about their democratic potential.

Nonetheless, I would also argue, the 'democratic' part of the 'democratainment' neologism is an occasional and accidental consequence of the 'entertainment' part, and its least systemic component. It is important to remember that celebrity still remains a systematically hierarchical and exclusive category, no matter how much it proliferates. No amount of public participation in game shows, reality TV or DIY celebrity web-sites will alter the fact that, overall, the media industries still remain in control of the symbolic economy, and that they still strive to operate this economy in the service of their own interests. Overwhelmingly now (and this has accelerated dramatically in recent years as governments' support for public broadcasting, in particular, has declined) these interests are commercial. It is worth stating that this fact alone should give us pause in suggesting they might also be democratic, simply because they have multiplied the range of choices available to the consumer. Robert McChesney's historical research into the debates about the introduction of commercial broadcasting into the United States in the 1930s provides us with a useful reminder that there is no natural connection between the commercial media and a democratic politics:

> Few people thought at the time that corporate-owned, advertising-supported broadcasting was the natural American system. That came later, when the PR industry went into fifth gear after the system was consolidated. Commercial broadcasting certainly was not regarded as inherently democratic. (As the BBC put it at the time, the claim by capitalist broadcasters that commercial broadcasting was democratic was 'outside our comprehension' and, as the BBC politely put it, 'clearly springs from a peculiarly American conception of democracy'.) (2007: 104)

Consequently, and while I might sympathize with more optimistic accounts, I also want to insist that there is no necessary connection between, on the one hand, a broadening demographic in the pattern of access to media representation and, on the other hand, a democratic politics. Diversity is not of itself intrinsically democratic irrespective of how it is generated or by whom. Hence, it is my view that these developments are more correctly described as a demotic, rather than a democratic, turn.

In a recent article, Nick Couldry and Tim Markham exposed an aspect of this issue to some detailed empirical examination.[5] As part of a broader research exercise, the Public Connection project (Couldry et al., 2007), they focused upon how 'celebrity culture … (as it intersects with the growth of reality TV, fashion culture and other areas of today's media cultures) offers connection to a world of politics and public issues' (2007: 404). Working with survey groups generating weekly diaries over a period of up to three months, the project developed data on 'media consumption, attitudes to media and politics, and public actions, and also the contexts in which all of these occur' (ibid: 407). The diarists' accounts indicated that celebrity culture did not seem to connect them with public issues, and subsequent analysis of the groups who made up what the research nominated as the 'celebrity cluster' revealed that this part of the sample was especially disengaged from public issues and questions of the public interest (as they were defined by the project). While the quantity of this group's media consumption was close to the average, there were some clear signs of significant differences in how they made use of it:

> Some 25% fewer respondents in the celebrity cluster, compared with the traditional cluster, feel a sense of duty to keep up with what's going on in the world … It is thus the lack of engagement with news, in parallel with a lack of social and political engagement [in terms of their personal and leisure activities], rather than lack of exposure to news … which marks the celebrity cluster as distinct. (ibid: 417)

The research is quite detailed and I am reluctant to rob it of its specificities and nuances by dealing with it too quickly here, but the conclusion of the article makes the point that we need to be careful about how confidently we can rely on any 'presumptions about the resonance of celebrity narratives for whole populations' (ibid: 418). Indeed, as Couldry and Markham report, there was considerable discussion in the diaries which could be interpreted as 'commentary on how irrelevant [celebrities] were to genuine public issues' (ibid: 418). Moreover, in the researchers' view, some of the more optimistic readings of the consumption of celebrity as constituting a kind of DIY political activity are very much wide of the mark:

> Those who followed celebrity culture were those least likely to be politically engaged. This is of course not surprising, and is certainly linked to the gendering of political culture, itself an important and socially regressive factor. Indeed, all the evidence suggests that following celebrity culture represents a positive choice by this group … Our argument is not … that there is anything 'wrong' with this choice, since such a choice can only be evaluated in the context of the wider gendering and polarization of the UK public sphere. Our point is rather that there is little evidence for some optimistic claims that this aspect of popular culture provides any potential routes into political culture, even in an expanded sense. If people's engagement with celebrity culture is part of a turning *away* from concern with issues that require public resolution (away from, in our definition, 'public connection'), then no amount of well-crafted messages will make a difference. (ibid: 418, emphasis in original)

As a result, the authors say the research does raise questions about the 'problematic relation between celebrity culture's "demotic turn" and actual prospects for democratic renewal and political change' (ibid: 418).

Producing ordinary identities

If the demotic turn is not producing democracy, then what is it doing? This is not an easy question to answer, and each chapter in this book will have its own angle from which it will try to respond. To start at the simplest level, though, we can say that it is generating content – a lot of content. What the media have to gain from their mining of the rich seam of 'the ordinary' is, at the very least, unlimited performances of diversity. Performing ordinariness has become an end in itself, and thus a rich and (or so it seems) almost inexhaustible means of generating new content for familiar formats. A number of media (television, radio, the internet) have developed production techniques which help to ensure that 'reality' is satisfactorily performed by the ordinary citizen even when their 'ordinariness' – given the processes of selection through which they have had to progress – is at least debatable. One of the means through which these processes are sanitized (that is, through which their implicit hierarchies are disavowed) is by dramatizing the democratizing implications of, for instance, the thousands of ordinary (that is, apparently untalented) applicants turning up to audition for *Idol*. Clearly, the visual spectacle of the audition tells us that anyone has a chance in such a competition. The *vox pop* interviews with various hopefuls which usually make up the first episode of the format reinforce this perception. It is in the interests of those who operate the hierarchy of celebrity in this context to mask its exclusivity in practice, and one of the distinguishing features of the demotic turn may well be the media industries' enhanced capacity to do this convincingly today. As we have seen, this enhanced capacity has dramatically increased the numbers of ordinary people it can attract and process.

There is more to this, however, and at this point I want to ask how we might think through the implications of what I have been describing. My motivation for asking this question is my sense that we are witnessing the emergence of a role for the media that is slightly different from the one which has been conventionally assumed within the traditional versions of media and communications studies (and more on that in a moment). Importantly, I suspect this is an aspect of the media's contemporary cultural influence which is new. In a conversation about these emerging forms of cultural influence, Chris Rojek once suggested to me that we may need to rethink the notion of the media as a 'mediating' apparatus because the media were operating in ways that were analogous to those we might once have attributed to the state: that is, as a source of power which now, rather than simply mediating between interests, organizes representations in support of their own interests. I thought then, and want to argue now, that there are good reasons why it might be useful to follow that suggestion to see where it leads us: to think about the media more in the way we have become accustomed to thinking about the state – as an apparatus with its own interests, and its own use for power.[6]

Let me clarify the distinction I am attempting to make here – and since it is a heuristic move rather than a substantive case I want to put forward, so I will acknowledge that this next set of explanations is a little crude. What I am trying to do is to compare conventional academic accounts of the media with the kinds of understandings that now seem necessary in response to what, I am arguing, are new and important developments. Let us think back a decade or two, to the conventional arguments we used in media and cultural studies to explain the relation between the media and the state. According to most models, the media were thought to operate as a medium or a carrier rather than as a motivating ideological force; their activities were the product of the interests of other locations of power: the state, largely, or perhaps capital. This reflected earlier versions of the political economies of the media industries, in which media industries were, in principle, independent in relation to the state but also to business. The media typically 'mediated' between the locations of power and their subjects. Among our original tasks in cultural studies was to interpret how the media did this in order to determine whose interests were being served and to what ends. We argued that we could use media texts as a means of accessing that information. Rarely (if ever) did we suggest that the texts merely served the interests of the media organizations themselves, although neither did we suggest that the media were always innocent of the uses to which these were put. Mostly, the media were framed as an instrument of the 'ideological state apparatuses' (if it wasn't an ISA itself), or of the nation-state, or of dominant ideological formations/power blocs, or even of the government – contingently and conjuncturally defined. We did not expect the media to simply serve their own interests (and I suspect that we doubted they could).

Moreover, and despite the structural importance of capital to the theoretical models which enabled this kind of commentary, I don't remember too many analyses in which commercial power was offered as the media's ultimate objective – even (I am surprised to recall) when we examined issues such as ownership and control. On the contrary, much of the discussion of the media during the 1970s and 1980s, including that of the concentration of media ownership, seemed to suggest that commercial power was itself only a means to an end: it had to be reducible to something else, something more fundamentally or structurally political, such as class interests or other forms of political or cultural hegemony.

The general point I want to make is that during these earlier formulations, we were interested in media texts for what they told us about the generation of meaning, and in media institutions for what they told us about the production of culture, but we tended not to look at the media as a primary motivating force – as themselves, the authors rather than the mediators of cultural identity. Even when we looked at public service broadcasters and their participation in the construction of national identity, we would normally have examined how individual programmes or network positioning constructed such identities as a means of accessing an ideological cultural or political agenda that was outside of and larger than the programming or its carrier.

Internationally, over the last decade or so, the media landscape has changed in ways that now significantly affect the nature of the media's involvement in the construction of cultural identities. Some of the relevant changes are in those markets where public service broadcasters have been displaced by a commercial and, often, a transnational media organization. Typically, where this occurs, the commercial provider attempts to appropriate the functions of the 'national' service, including the construction of citizenship or of membership to the state or national community. In Australia, the market I know best, the leading commercial network (whichever it is) loses no opportunity to stake their claim to being 'the national broadcaster', notwithstanding the fact that there is still a publicly-funded national broadcaster with a national network that is far greater in size and reach, if not in audience ratings, than any of the commercial networks. The point of such a claim, in this instance at least, is primarily commercial – or, more correctly, it serves as a means of extending the network's social and political purchase in order to extend their commercial power. While there may well be ideological consequences to flow from a move such as this, they are by-products rather than a primary concern.

The identities constructed by the media networks I am referring to here are, I would argue, not merely 'mediated'; as I have been suggesting, sometimes they are constructed from whole cloth. Although I would accept the possibility that this observation might apply to public or national identities as well, my primary focus here is on the media's construction of the private identity: the personal, the ordinary and the everyday. It is not difficult to see how the demotic turn collaborates with this. In its most vivid location, the hybrid reality TV/game-show franchise, the production of celebrity promises a spectacular form of personal validation.[7] Paradoxically, the format's apparent tolerance of a lack of exceptional talents or achievements is available as long as the person concerned can perform their ordinariness with some degree of specificity or individuality. Reality TV of this kind issues an open invitation to its participants to merge their personal everyday reality with that created publicly by television. The fact that the opportunity is offered and accepted as a validating or empowering process for the 'actual' (as well as the televisually performing) individual shrinks the distance between these two dimensions of everyday life – 'on-television' and 'not-on-television' – even though everyone is thoroughly aware of how constructed the process actually is.

Nick Couldry has provided us with a resonant explanation of the appeal of such a process in his description of the place the media occupy within systems of identity and desire among many of our citizens. Couldry's 'myth of the media centre' refers to what he describes as the commonly held belief that there is a centre to the social world and that, in some sense, the media speak from and for that centre (2003: 46). As a result, there are media people and there are ordinary people; crossing the boundary which separates these two categories of person takes one from the periphery to the centre of the social. In the context I am addressing here, the myth of the media centre has been useful to the media industries because it legitimates formations of identity that are primarily invented in order to generate commercial returns. That is, what Couldry sees as the media's perceived social centrality is an effect of an apparatus that has built the media's power, but as a commercial rather than an ideological or political imperative. This is why I am so interested in the extent to which we might argue that the media now play a significantly different role in inventing, popularizing and distributing formations of identity and desire in our societies. The implications of this argument are fairly plain, I would have thought. If the media operate in order to seem like the 'natural representatives of society's centre' (Couldry, 2003: 46), and if they occupy the centre of symbolic production, then the kinds of realities they offer as forms of identity within their programming must have a powerful social and cultural impact. That is the situation to which I am responding.

The media and their interests

Among my responses is to point out that the impact of these new forms of identity seems out of all proportion to the motivations which call them into being. This is not necessarily a critique of what they are, but the scale and penetration of their circulation prompt me to go back to that earlier question – just what kind of cultural apparatus are the media these days? Another way of framing that concern might go like this. What do we make of a situation where a powerful mechanism of legitimation is being mobilized in ways with which we are familiar from other projects – in the service of the construction of the citizenry, for instance, or in developing plausible demonstrations of the homogeneity of the nation – in order to represent forms of behaviour and identity that are motivated simply by a particular business's need to establish their viability as commercial entertainment or spectacle? To address that question (and it is important we do so given its wholesale intervention into the formations of cultural identity today, particularly among the young), perhaps we should be asking some slightly old-fashioned questions of the media as a formation, that is, asking not just in whose interests they operate but what might constitute the media's own interests.

However, I am not going to do that right now. At this point in the conversation, I need to say that I actually don't yet think the media do work exactly like a state, even though this is a helpful way to resituate our thinking about the kind of social and cultural apparatus they have lately become. As a strategy, it does assist in focusing on the media's behaviour and on what that behaviour tells us about the media's objectives and interests. What I notice about the behaviour of the media system I am describing is that it seems utterly short term in its concentration on producing the conditions for commercial success and shamelessly contingent in the tactics chosen to pursue that outcome. In the instances upon which I have been focusing, that means something apparently quite banal: generating audience and participant behaviours which will result in successful television entertainment programmes. Less banal, though, is the possibility that these behaviours, where they occur, are nonetheless the result of a direct and sustained intervention into the construction of people's desires, cultural identities and expectations of the real. As we shall see in the discussion of reality TV in Chapter 2, their effect is not only to generate thousands of applications to appear on *Big Brother* or *Pop Idol*; other effects also spill out beyond the boundaries of the programme as largely uncontained and so far relatively uninspected by-products. As a result, current research[8] is reporting that 'becoming famous' is now being talked about as a realistic career option by young people even though they have yet to decide in what area of public performance they might pursue their fame. All of that said, the curious thing is that the behaviours we have been discussing seem to have no intrinsic content or necessary politics. I suspect that there is no reason why an entirely different format would not drive entirely different behaviours or be mobilized to generate completely different constructions of cultural identity. Yet I would also accept that it would not be difficult to extract a set of principles of citizenship or an implied and contingent ethical framework underpinning the structure and narrativization of much contemporary reality programming; as will become clear from a more developed discussion in the following chapter, I am not suggesting that this is without its own internal argument.

In this chapter so far, I have been raising what seem to be important implications to draw from the rise of a media formation generating behaviours and cultural patterns that reinforce its commercial power and its cultural centrality within a changing public sphere, but the actual content of which is driven (at least in the first instance) by the needs of an entertainment format. It is a system that could be described as operating like an ideological system but without an ideological project. I am proposing that there is now a new dimension of cultural power available to the international media system, and that it has the capacity not only to generate celebrity identities from whole cloth but it may also have the capacity to generate broader formations of cultural identity from whole cloth as well. The media system I am describing is largely multinational or transnational in its semiotic reach and economic organization, but relatively localized in its application, purchase and effects. The design and distribution of formats are locally differentiated and so the effects often are too. However, while the interest in generating the behaviours and audiences I am talking about might be highly localized in terms of specific ratings wars in specific markets, for instance, the celebrity of the formats themselves is increasingly globalized. This suits the large media conglomerates who have learned how to trade their formats across cultural and national differences, but it also means that they may be trading in constructions of identity that are dislocated from any social or cultural context. As we shall see in Chapter 2, that can raise some challenging issues when, for instance, western formats are taken up in non-western locations in ways that immediately generate controversies about their effects on local cultural practices. Interestingly, and to qualify this, there are also many examples of local versions which have modified formats to give them a degree of indigeneity that reverses the flow of globalization, suggesting there is no standard formula to help us understand the basic coordinates of this transaction (Roscoe, 2001a).

Notwithstanding that qualification, the alarming and perhaps surprising thing for someone working in cultural or media studies today is that the forms of cultural identity the media produce are so contingent, that they are so loosely connected to the social conditions from which they emerge, and that they are the object of so little sense of responsibility from those who generated them in the first place. As a result, rather than an increase in access providing the route to a more representative and coherent expression of the will and ambition of the people (which is what we might have hoped), there is a sense in which the demotic turn has unleashed the unruly, unpredictable and irresponsible characteristics of Le Bon's (1960 [1901]) nineteenth-century crowd – the true sense of the demotic in all its unharnessable, exciting but anarchic character: energetic, over-responsive, excessive and capable of instigating but not easily organizing or managing social and cultural change (Marshall, 1997: see Chapter 2).

I am, of course, aware that these are also the very characteristics upon which the conservative taste-based critiques of *Big Brother* and similar popular programmes have focused: it is easy to slide into this kind of position. My interest in this is not to pursue that taste-based critique, however. Instead my interest lies in what the success of the demotic turn says about the cultural and industrial formation that produced it, and about the kinds of effects this formation may generate in the future. Before going much further, however, I need to flesh these interests out just a little by attempting to clarify the differences between the kind of enquiry that I am prosecuting here, and those more conventional, more moralistic, critiques responding to the widespread phenomenon of 'tabloidization' over the last decade or so – the years of the demotic turn.

Tabloidization

The notion of tabloidization, together with its associated 'laments' (Langer, 1998) and rationalizations (Hartley, 1996), has been around academic discussions of the media for quite some time. It was initially located in 1990s' discussions of shifts in the definitions of 'what counts' as news and current affairs, in which most news outlets (not just those seen to be at the lower end of the taste or 'quality' scale) are widely thought to have headed in the following direction:

> ... away from politics and towards crime, away from the daily news agenda and towards editorially generated items

promoted days in advance, away from information-based treatments of social issues and towards entertaining stories on lifestyles or celebrities, and [finally towards] an overwhelming investment in the power of the visual, in the news as an entertaining spectacle. (Turner, 1999: 59)

The notion grew, however, from this kind of specific application to the point where the label of tabloidization was expanded to cover a 'broad-based cultural movement', that was not only evident in media forms but also in the wider culture. Typically, such an application was marked by the 'increasing commercialization of modern life and a corresponding decline in "traditional values"' (ibid: 60). As a result, the term was widely (and readily) deployed by those who wanted to criticize the behaviours and moralities of the popular media and popular culture in general. Indeed, in an earlier discussion of the phenomenon, I noted the political difficulties cultural studies faced in itself criticizing any of the forms and practices which had become the focus of the tabloidization critique: 'given [this critique's] compatibility with elitist and conservative readings of popular culture', I argued, 'aligning oneself in agreement with any one of its criticisms is to risk being aligned with the whole agenda' (1999: 68). Furthermore, I suggested, the phenomenon of tabloidization had now become 'implausibly inclusive': 'it incorporates lifestyle programming, advice columns in newspapers, afternoon talk shows, viewer video formats, hidden camera journalism, gossip magazines, and much more, into a miscellany of symptoms for a cultural malaise' (ibid.). Consequently, at that time, I took the view that the category was not an enabling one for the kinds of analysis and critique that needed to be done: it was 'too baggy, imprecise and value-laden to be of any use ... in attempting to understand the appeal and cultural function' of the kinds of tendencies I had been examining in contemporary news and current affairs (ibid: 70).

The category has stuck around, nevertheless, although in its most recent formations it has been much more explicit about its penetration into discussions of changes in the public sphere more generally and about its migration from the original focus on the news media. Martin Conboy's foreword to one of the most recent and developed accounts of tabloidization (importantly, it is not 'tabloidization' any longer, but 'tabloid culture') acknowledges this connection when he notes how 'tabloid values have come to permeate our general media culture' (2008: xv). The editors of *The Tabloid Culture Reader*, Anita Biressi and Heather Nunn, point out that tabloidization was itself originally 'a tabloid term': 'a media industry expression rather than a scholarly concept, denoting a dumbing down of media content and a weakening of the *ideal* functions of mass media in liberal democracies' (emphasis in original). As they go on to say, echoing my earlier point, while it was 'originally deployed to describe a decline in journalistic standards [tabloidizaton] is now increasingly applied to all forms of mainstream media content including talk shows and radio phone-ins, reality television, gross-out comedy, celebrity magazines and even documentary' (2008: 1).

The term, then, has had to do a lot of work, in the context of academic debate, that it was never intended to do. That said, it has been widely and enthusiastically taken up. However, it could be argued that the breadth of its application indicates, on the one hand, how eagerly sections of the community have appropriated it to their own interests rather than, on the other hand, testifying to the precision or accuracy with which it might isolate and identify the characteristics in question. As a term that might be useful within academic debate, it probably never really had that much to offer and so it is not surprising that Biressi and Nunn choose the phrase 'tabloid culture' as their preferred alternative. Rather than focusing attention on a particular market or a particular taste-based media form, they see this choice of descriptor as a means of denoting 'the newer formations of media culture that draw together ... so many of the features that were commonly attributed to older tabloid formats' (ibid.). It is a strategy that I can understand; it seems to me, too, that there are clearly common elements in the current formations of media cultures that we need to examine as a cultural conjuncture rather than as disaggregated analyses of particular media or selected attributes of their formats.

Biressi and Nunn are careful to point to the long history of the tabloid press, going back to nineteenth-century newspapers in Britain and the USA, before moving on to analyses of its more contemporary formations. They pick up common elements in the accounts of the tabloid press that appear increasingly from the 1970s onwards, and that draw attention to the 'tightening bond between entertainment industries, consumerism and the tabloid press', as well as to the kinds of content that are associated with the 'tabloid profile': 'sexual vulgarity, the use of popular vernacular, and a radical iconoclastic conservatism' aimed at capturing the attention of a 'non-elite audience' (ibid: 9). Fundamental to the critical response to the growth of this profile across media formats, they argue, was the proposition that it constituted a clear demonstration that the media had surrendered their fourth estate principles to an unrestrained commercialism, pandering to the 'lowest common denominator in order to sell copy and support a free-market ethos':

> As such it may be regarded as a process that inexorably erodes serious journalism across all spheres, genres, and platforms such as radio and broadcast news, documentary, political reportage and online journalism. Debate about tabloidization therefore necessarily addresses the tensions between entertainment and information within an increasingly multimedia and globalized consumer environment. (ibid: 10)

While their collection, as a whole, is appropriately ecumenical about the social and political effects of this, it is the pervasiveness of tabloid culture and its steady migration from its original, specific, media locations that seem to interest them most.

The extent of the pervasiveness of tabloid culture and thus its implications can, of course, be exaggerated. Accounts of tabloidization in the 1990s, such as Franklin's (1998) discussion of 'newszak', could lead to the perception that there was an irresistible juggernaut of bad taste levelling the media landscape everywhere you went. The 1980s–1990s' sprint downmarket was certainly not an exercise in which everybody participated, nor was it the same in every location. Rather, its effects were uneven and significantly market-contingent. In Australia, for example, most of the metropolitan tabloid newspapers had actually disappeared by the end of the twentieth century, while the 'quality' end of the market continued to thrive. Although the provision of (and the audiences for) broadcast news and current affairs has declined dramatically in the UK, for instance, the increased amount of news available through

24-hour subscription and online news services could be argued to more than compensate for that. The rise of the news blog (and we will be looking at this in more detail in Chapter 3), the conventional example used to provide evidence for the expansion of a newly democratic public sphere, does seem directly related to the concentration of news media organizations and their dominance of broadcasting and other mass media news. And while it might be true that broadcast television's political coverage has declined in many markets most of the time, more than 70 million US viewers watched the Biden–Palin US Vice-Presidential debate on 3 October 2008, making it the second most watched political debate ever (coming in behind the 80 million people who watched the Carter–Reagan debate in 1980). As Toby Miller (2009) has demonstrated, television was still emphatically the main game for those who wanted to follow the 2008 presidential election campaigns. This is a reminder that we need to keep our eyes on the details as we try to understand these trends.

In terms of tabloid culture's regimes of taste – the so-called vulgarization of the media, for instance – it is important to acknowledge that there is a significant dimension of popular media content that sets out to offend middle-class standards of taste as a deliberate commercial and discursive strategy, not as the inadvertent or ill-informed consequence of a 'failure' of taste. Jane Shattuc's (1998) discussion of US TV's day-time talk shows described conservative media criticism of programmes such as that hosted by Ricki Lake as an attempt to bully the popular audience into adopting more middle-class standards of taste – something that would have these audience members accepting the denigration, repression and subordination of precisely the regimes of value which rule much of their own everyday lives. She argues that those whose favourite programmes are the targets of such critiques are not unaware of this; hence their adoption of a mode of consumption which does not so much fail to perform in ways that fit with the tastes of their critics as deliberately set out to offend them (cf. Turner, 1999: 72–4). A similar line of argument is developed by Bev Skeggs in her (2005) discussion of the audience for *Wife Swap* which is taken up in the following chapter.

Biressi and Nunn's focus on 'tabloid culture' takes them away from such class- and taste-based critiques towards a consideration of what might be the social and cultural implications of the media shifts they bring together by way of that label. From such a point of view, they imply, the conventional 'tabloidization' critique is in many ways simply beside the point. Furthermore, they are sympathetic to the argument that some of the shifts collected under the label of the tabloid have been significantly inclusive in their use of 'non-elite people, issues and values'. The possibility that this might constitute a form of democratic participation needs to be taken seriously:

> It could be said that the relationship between 'the popular' and 'the public sphere' has taken a new turn with the advent of first-person media and reality television leading critics to test and sometimes explicitly challenge outright condemnations of tabloid culture ... Many of these arguments emerge from the conviction that even the most denigrated forms of popular culture need to be engaged with at a serious academic level; not merely as vehicles of commercialism and ideological persuasion but also as potential sites of cultural struggle, transgressive pleasures and media visibility for ordinary people and common culture. (2008: 10)

All of that seems eminently sensible and appropriate to me. I am not entirely convinced, though, that the idea of the tabloid gives me the best means of prosecuting the engagement they describe. In particular, its roots in a form of motivated political critique, and the inescapable fact that the judgments involved in deciding what is part of the tabloid and what isn't (who determines what constitutes vulgarity, for instance?) are hopelessly overdetermined by class, gender and other factors, make it highly unstable territory from which to launch the kind of enquiry I have in mind for this book. So, while some of what I want to examine in this book could be located within what Biressi and Nunn call tabloid culture, it is not 'tabloid-ness' that ultimately interests me. Rather, when I examine the popular success of reality TV, of talkback radio, of political blogs, of online journalism, of user-generated content on the Web and of social networking sites, I am interested in understanding what function these media forms have for their participants – the 'housemates', the callers, the bloggers, the posters of comments, the online friends – as well as for those consumers who simply watch, read or listen. I am interested in these functions as the signs of an expanded role for a comprehensively commercialized media in constructing cultural identities through new, often participatory and interactive, forms of entertainment across a broad range of media platforms and formats.

My first port of call, in the following chapter, is to take a much closer look at this through reality TV.

Notes

1 This is an expanded version of the material originally published in the *International Journal of Cultural Studies* (2006, 9(2): 153–66) as 'The mass production of celebrity: celetoids, reality TV and the "demotic turn"'.

2 Su Holmes (2005) has an excellent discussion of *Big Brother*, ordinariness and celebrity in Holmes and Jermyn (2005). While her concerns are ultimately quite different to mine, a number of the issues dealt with here are also raised in hers.

3 Nick Couldry has made the point to me that we know very little about to what extent this appetite is 'industry constructed' rather than the product of some kind of grassroots cultural process (which is how it is customarily understood). It is a fair point and, like him, I am unaware of any empirical work on this area which could answer that question.

4 See Chapter 3 in my *Understanding Celebrity*. This is in fact a common theme in many accounts of contemporary TV, such as Bonner's *Ordinary Television* (2003), Dovey's *Freakshow* (2000) or the many accounts of reality TV formats such as *Big Brother*. The core location to which I am referring, however, is the 'GirlCultures' project currently being conducted by Catharine Lumby and Elspeth Probyn, which is reporting clear evidence of this from their interviews with teenage girls in Sydney. At this stage, most of this work has only appeared in conference presentations rather than in print, but it is referenced in Lumby (2003).

5 Nick Couldry and Tim Markham (2007) 'Celebrity culture and public connection: bridge or chasm?', *International Journal of Cultural Studies*, 10(4) December: 403–22.

6 Nick Couldry also investigates the idea of the media as a quasi-state, in different and interesting ways, in his 'Media meta-capital: extending the range of Bourdieu's field theory' (2004).

7 This is also a point well made at some length in Holmes (2005).

8 See note 3.

2

Reality TV and the Construction of Cultural Identities

The cultural function of reality TV

Reality TV, regarded as an aggregation of its various iterations, may well be the most exorbitantly 'noticed' form of programming in television's history. Operating, as it does, in such an ongoing, complex, and problematically mediated relation to its audience's everyday lives, reality TV might range from the provocative to the boring, the engaging or the repellent, but it can certainly attract attention. Indeed it has attracted its critics and its defenders in about equal measure. The formats usually included under this label have a quite varied relation to 'the real': some are highly narrativized and mediated, some are actually just updated game shows for whom the 'reality' descriptor is more an indicator of format style than any claim to be capturing real life, and still others are essentially documentary in their format and in their ethical relation to the material they put before viewers. Gathered together, they constitute a major shift in how television content has been produced, traded and consumed over the last decade or so. My interest in this chapter, though, is focused on reality TV's cultural function – both for the audiences and for the participants.

In terms of the nature of the content this shift has produced, it seems undeniable that, through these formats, ordinary people have gained unprecedented access to representation in the media. Many would argue, however, that this has not necessarily benefited those ordinary people. Indeed, as these formats developed, television producers stumbled upon a new industrial strategy for turning ordinary people into marketable celebrity-commodities – Chris Rojek's (2001) 'celetoids': they enjoy exceptional visibility over short periods of time, but their public careers are almost entirely articulated to the needs of the media organization which produced them. The perceived constructed-ness and the demonstrably brief life of this celebrity – that is, what the format actually proves to offer as an outcome of this new access and visibility – have provoked a great deal of debate about the 'reality' of reality TV, as well as about its cultural function. The debates about its cultural function situate themselves somewhere on a continuum between two opposing points of view. At one end, there are those who see reality TV as a taste-less and cynical exploitation of ordinary people's interest in becoming famous, on the one hand, and the contemporary audience's regrettable fascination with witnessing spectacles of shame and humiliation, on the other. At the opposite end, there are those who regard reality TV as a positively empowering development which has opened the media up to new participants in ways that mirror the democratization so often attributed to the digital revolution and the rise of Web 2.0.[1]

As Annette Hill has reported from her recent research among UK audiences, it is common even for those who watch reality TV regularly to describe it frankly as 'crap' (2008: 105). The mainstream media themselves, even while they profit from publishing the latest news from programmes or gossip about one of their celebrities, routinely attack reality TV for its crassness and happily describe it as the nadir of contemporary entertainment. This is a taste- and class-based critique, designed to reflect the class and generational inflections of this opinion within the population. That such an opinion is out there seems beyond question. There are now a number of research projects which have picked up the older generation's particular distaste for reality TV (Bennett et al., 2009; Hill, 2008), as well as the more general class-based assessment of your typical reality TV participants as examples of what has come to be labelled in the UK and the USA, unfortunately, as 'white trash celebrity'.

There is, of course, a great deal of hypocrisy in the print media's performance of disdain for reality TV. The survival of the mass market magazine and of the tabloid newspaper typified by the British market's 'redtops' or the USA's *National Enquirer* is structurally dependent on the expanded interest in celebrity right across the media landscape. In the UK, especially, the print media are heavily reliant upon the television industry's investment in the systematic production of celebrities through reality TV. Typically, the mode of print media reporting employed in recounting the latest story from, say, *Big Brother*, has it both ways: it is able to recount a story to its supposedly disapproving but nonetheless attentive readers in scandalous detail, while at the same time taking the moral high ground by deploring the programme involved and treating the personalities it creates with contempt. The career of former UK *Big Brother* contestant Jade Goody, for instance, provided the print media in the UK and elsewhere with an enormous amount of material upon which they could mount their critique not only of that programme, and reality TV in general, but also of her personally.[2] In 2008, Goody was appearing in the Indian version of *Big Brother* (called *Bigg Boss*) when she was informed by her doctor that she had been diagnosed with a form of cancer – live, on screen, as part of the entertainment. It is not surprising that this should be criticized as tasteless and exploitative but, in one instance at least, the critique of this failure of taste had its own failures. Rod Liddle's (2008) column dealing with this in *The Spectator* was headlined: 'After Jade's cancer, what next? "I'm a tumour, get me out of here?"' As a media performance, that headline (and most of what was published beneath it) is as tasteless and as insensitive in its treatment of the *Big Brother* ex-housemate as the behaviour it purports to criticize.[3]

That said, it would be wrong to simply dismiss the criticism of reality TV as solely driven by a conservative, middle-class distaste for excessive forms of popular culture (although it certainly includes that dimension). These programmes' treatment of their celebrity-commodities is open to other kinds of concern. There is plenty of evidence that, in at least some of the bigger global formats, contestants have been trapped within contractual obligations that are exploitative by anyone's standards.[4] Sue Collins (2008) has reported that the contractual arrangement for contestants on *Survivor* cedes to the US television network CBS the right to restrict any media contact, celebrity work or appearances for up to three years after the series goes on air. In addition, 'the contract includes a "life story rights" section that effectively binds the signatory into relinquishing control over his or her life story and public image' (2008: 98), virtually in perpetuity. The network is able to get away with this kind of thing because these celebrities, unlike other kinds of celebrities such as actors who play fictional characters in multiple vehicles, derive all of their public visibility from this one vehicle. While they have, of course, willingly accepted such a contract, their power to leverage a better deal at the beginning is minimal given the huge number of equally qualified contestants waiting in the wings to take their place; later on, once they have built a following, it is simply too late. The point Collins makes is that these contestants are caught within a power structure that is far more heavily weighted against their interests than is the case for more conventional types of performer. As I put it in my discussion of this issue in *Understanding Celebrity* (Turner, 2004: 54), 'these celebrities are especially dependent upon the program that made them visible in the first place; they have virtually no other platform from which to address their audience'. Furthermore, they have good reason for wishing to continue to honour the contract long after a series has aired. Certain long-running formats – among them *Survivor, Real World* and *Celebrity Big Brother* – have return opportunities for favourite contestants, high-profile evictees and the like.

The commodification of these contestants is relentless, even though the continuing success of the format depends on their expendability; it is important that they are easily replaced by the next series' crop of contenders. My own research for *Understanding Celebrity* brought me into contact with several former contestants from *Big Brother Australia* and from the New Zealand originated format, *Popstars*, who told stories about being grossly misled about their career prospects before the show was produced, caricatured while the show was on air, and offered only those opportunities which would promote the franchise or the network after the show was completed.[5] While the contestants I talked to had gone into the experience seeking a career outcome and not merely celebrity, that career outcome was not delivered. Mark Andrejevic (2004) reported similar findings from his much more systematic research among a larger group of contestants from MTV's *Real World*. The extent to which contestants in these formats believe they have been misled by producers was indeed among the questions pursued by an early British inquiry into reality TV, published as the *Consenting Adults* report (Hibbard et al., 2000). The fact that such a question was asked reflects the view that contestants are in a poor position to provide informed consent because they have so little understanding of, or control over, how they will be represented during and after a programme. Their disempowered status was considered in the report as a problem to be addressed by public regulation.

There is also another – perhaps an obvious – dimension, which relates to the fact that so much of reality television is devoted to the exposure, humiliation and shaming of its contestants. Annette Hill's research is extremely interesting in this regard because it found that the audiences she surveyed responded in ambivalent ways to this: many would continue to watch material that they found embarrassing and repellent, while nonetheless feeling some guilt and shame at their own complicity. That does not stop these audience members, however, from criticizing the contestants for exposing themselves to such a situation, thus reflecting the often very negative views expressed about reality TV participants in general. Nonetheless, it is not surprising that criticism of reality TV programmes which involve humiliation of some kind or another should provoke the question: what do these programmes say about the society that chooses to watch them for entertainment? I don't have an answer to this, although I have certainly experienced the discomfort implied by such a question. However, it is worth noting Annette Hill's use of Elspeth Probyn's (2005) connection between shame and 'interest'. Probyn, she says, claims that 'shame illuminates our intense attachment to the world, our desire to be connected with others, and the knowledge that, as merely human, we will sometimes fail in our attempts to maintain those connections' (Hill, 2008: 196). Looked at in this way, Hill proposes, shame is not 'only a negative emotion, but rather an uncomfortable, sometimes hurtful, emotion, which alerts us to what is important in our lives' (ibid.). Nonetheless, it is hard to see our enjoyment of that emotion, our seeking it out for entertainment, as a positive thing.

More worrying, and something we will return to later on in this chapter, is, again perhaps, one of the more obvious sources of discomfort for the many who are offended by the whole premise underlying *Big Brother*, in particular: the cheeky and iconoclastic appropriation of what was once the marker of a powerful political critique of the authoritarian society that turns into the heavily ironic title of a format of popular entertainment. In the process, of course, the key practice of authoritarian surveillance is stripped of its political salience in order to maximize the entertainment value of its voyeuristic deployment. The *Big Brother* reference has become so benign, so dissociated from its Orwellian roots, that contestants compete fiercely for the chance to perform what Mark Andrejevic (2004) has described as 'the work of being watched'. Again, and notwithstanding their willingness to perform such work, Andrejevic questions the participants' understanding of the power relations involved. Drawing parallels between the contestants in a reality programme such as *Big Brother* or *Real World*, and the webcam presence of a Jennifer Ringley, he says:

> Conceived of as a form of work, the activity of being watched can be described in terms of differential access to the means of surveillance and to the benefits that accrue to the exploitation of this labor. The operative question is not whether a particular conception of privacy has been violated but rather, what are the relations that underwrite entry into a relationship of surveillance, and who profits from the work of being watched? (2004: 79)

Of course, the producers take a very different view on such issues. Their rhetoric is either tuned towards asking people to lighten up and recognize that this is just a piece of harmless entertainment, on the one hand, or towards pointing to the controversies generated by these more provocative formats as constituting a public service of highlighting public debate on important social issues, on the other (see, for instance, Endemol producer Peter Bazelgette's book [2005]). Hence, Jade Goody's live diagnosis might have raised public awareness of the dangers of cancer among young people, or her abuse of Bollywood star Shilpa Shetty in 2007 might have served the useful purpose of bringing issues of racism to the surface for public consideration. Certainly, there is plenty of evidence that the activities taking place during the production of such shows have been taken up as issues of intense public concern. The media panics around some of the European versions of *Big Brother* (such as the French version, *Loft Story*) framed the issues concerned as of general social and moral significance and not merely as of interest to media regulators (Biltereyst, 2005). In Australia, a controversy over an incident in which a female contestant was 'turkey slapped'[6] during *Big Brother* generated criticism from the Prime Minister at the time, the summary eviction of the two males concerned, massive public condemnation in the print media, and a broadcasting regulator's inquiry – even though the incident itself was not broadcast live (it was circulated online from the 24-hour feed and eventually picked up and broadcast by a current affairs programme on a rival television network). The generation of controversy is, of course, an effective strategy for building an audience; the greater the notoriety, in many cases, the higher the ratings. Confronted with such an accusation, the producers tend to point to the level of public concern as a vindication of their decision to make their 'contribution to public debate'.

That said, there are plenty of reality formats which have an explicitly public good or pedagogic purpose, and so it would be unfair to accuse all producers here of disingenuously claiming such a benefit where none exists. Formats such as *Supernanny*, *You Are What You Eat*, *How to Look Good Naked*, for instance (and whatever you might think of them as entertainment), all set out to produce what most would regard as better outcomes for their contestants while modelling appropriate behaviours for their viewers. (I will come back to this issue shortly.) Consequently, it is not surprising that there is a considerable body of academic opinion that aligns itself more or less with the industry's defence of the formats in arguing that even some of the more voyeuristic formats (*Big Brother*, certainly, but perhaps not *Temptation Island*) have a pedagogic dimension. Usually, this is attributed to the programmes' invitation to their audiences to engage freely in a fundamentally ethical critique of the behaviour they are witnessing (Hartley, 2008; Lumby, 2003; Skeggs et al., 2008). According to such arguments, the audience's consumption of the text typically involves assessing and judging the behaviours represented much as one would while observing the behaviour of one's acquaintances in everyday life. In this way, then, it is an extension of the experiences of everyday life. Furthermore, as a consequence of the format's standard claim to provide an unmediated representation of reality and the audience's demonstrable scepticism about the validity of that claim, reality TV's audiences are actively engaged in assessing its value. Rather than being passively consumed by its audiences, Hill (among others) suggests, 'reality TV invites a critical viewing mode' (2008: 140).

There is strong evidence from the audience research to support such suggestions. For Hill's research subjects, the programme *Wife Swap* operates as a source of 'people watching' for comparison and possible emulation (Hill, 2008: 200) as they learn about the 'differences between participants in the series and their incivility towards each other':

> In many ways it [*Wife Swap*] teaches us about negative emotions and what happens when these are not controlled or managed. It highlights how there are different feeling rules for parenting, with some parents teaching their children about emotion work, and others eschewing the management of emotions ... The comparative strategies for watching *Wife Swap* enable audiences to distance themselves from these kinds of people, and their ethical treatment of each other and by programme makers. (ibid.)

Skeggs et al. (2008: 13) report that their group of female, working-class research subjects, again viewing *Wife Swap*, adopted a position of moral authority while watching and commenting upon the text that had not been evident in earlier interviews with the research team. Theirs was not so much a reflexive commentary on the text as an active participation in it:

> The working class participants responded to the 'reality' television participants as if they were 'real' – not representations – and invested in moral positions related to their 'real' lives ... In this particular example [the episode of *Wife Swap*] participants from Brockley take the moral high ground in relation to parenting, demonstrating empathy and judgement through personal experience and ultimately *immanently positioning themselves* within the unfolding drama. They dramatically enact their own life choice – making maternal and domestic sacrifices for the family – as the right choice, displaying and authorizing their emotional labour. (2008: 13, emphasis in original)

The case for the pedagogic, critical and ethical function of these programme formats, I believe, is a convincing one and needs to inform our discussion of their cultural function in general. Surprisingly, perhaps, this aspect has also turned up in interviews with former contestants where even those who may have other reservations about their time on the show still talk about it as a learning experience – as a 'means of getting in touch with themselves and others' (Andrejevic, 2004: 108). Even more surprisingly, some connected this to the therapeutic benefits of surveillance, equating the 'willingness to be "open" on camera (that is, to submit oneself to comprehensive monitoring) with "being real", and consequently with personal growth' (ibid: 109).[7] The equation provides some insight into the kinds of individuality that are preferred (interestingly, by both the producers and the participants) as the products of this kind of experience.

While I accept the argument made for the role of ethical judgment in framing the participation of audiences in certain formats, this last set of claims – connecting empowerment with surveillance – is both a little alarming and, ultimately, difficult to take seriously. Mind you, the elicitation of disbelief and ambivalence is typical of our engagement with reality TV. For every argument that describes the opportunity provided to Jade Goody as a democratizing one, there is another which points to the cynical and exploitative way in which many of these opportunities have been distributed. (Casting, for instance, does tend to get more bizarre as the series move into successive iterations; in Australia, the final series of Big Brother included a belly-dancing dwarf who injured herself early on, in a task designed for a taller person, and took no further part in the series.) In fact, the ambivalence we might register about reality television does seem hardwired into the very things that make it most interesting to its audiences. Hill describes it in this way:

If reality performers are shamed and humiliated, then viewers also feel ashamed by their pleasure in watching. Their personal interest in seeing people put in emotionally difficult situations, in watching how shameless reality performers can be in their pursuit of fame, makes reality TV both attractive and repulsive to viewers. In some ways, viewers adopt a shallow ethical position, placing self-interest first, seeing reality TV participants as a resource to be managed for entertainment. In other ways, viewers adopt a deep ethical position, feeling guilty about the treatment of participants, and moving towards a more universal position on the rights of participants. (2008: 173–4)

Given such processes of consumption, it is little wonder there is a continuing conversation about what we might make of the cultural function of reality TV.

Reality TV and the demotic turn

Where does this place reality TV in relation to the demotic turn? In terms of the audience's engagement with the format, I believe it is clear that reality TV programmes in general have demonstrated an exceptional capacity to embed themselves in the processes through which their audiences construct their everyday lives. They have done this in ways that are significantly different from, say, fictional drama. As audiences participate in the process of making sense of these texts, they seem to do so with more confidence in their own authority, and in the moral, ethical and social judgments that this involves. This is not necessarily because reality TV formats are seen to be more authentic and thus more connected with everyday life; in fact, this claim appears to be treated with scepticism by most viewers. Rather, because these formats use a more or less plausible construction of everyday life as their explicit field of representation, they generate a mode of consumption that actively responds to the formats' invitation to regard the audiences' own judgments and responses as direct contributions to the meanings and pleasures of the programme. Sometimes, this is formalized to the extent that they are also contributing to the programme's narrative progress through SMS voting and so on.

In such respects, then, there is a genuine point to those arguments which claim that the format is inherently empowering for the ordinary viewer. Due to the fact that this is a more active relation to these programmes than is common with most other television formats, reality TV carries with it a sense of authenticity that is generated through the prosecution and/or resolution of a dialogue between the constructed 'reality' of a programme and that of a viewer's own life experience. At its most developed, this dialogue also includes interactions with other media – the internet, the mobile phone, and so on – and thus resembles an active participation in the programme itself more than is the case with anything previously provided on television. Through access to such programmes outside of the broadcast regimes (through online feeds, chat rooms, and so on), there is also the availability of an online fan, and a shared critical culture as well.

That said, or perhaps because of this, the format's capacity to generate such vigorous and multi-platformed activity, as well as its capacity to generate such public debate and controversy, is seen by some sections of the audience to be out of all proportion to the significance of the content it uses to attract an audience. For those who find reality TV thoroughly objectionable (and there are plenty who do), the format's apparent realism or claims to authenticity can be the very thing that provokes the most criticism: first, to deny its reality, salience and significance and then to vilify everyone who has had anything to do with it.[8]

One of the key provocations to the critics is the putative ordinariness of the participants. Not such a problem with the more documentary 'fly-on-the-wall' (or what in the UK tends to classify as a 'docu-soap') end of the format – programmes such as *Airport* or *Driving School* – this is clearly a major problem for the end that produces *Idol, Fame Academy, The X-Factor* or *Big Brother*. While their producers defend the democratic credentials even of these latter formats, speaking of them as an egalitarian means of providing open access to extremely competitive media careers (itself a questionable claim in terms of the outcomes for most participants), there are plenty who would make the point that there is always going to be a process of selection going on – even when choosing ordinary people. Frances Bonner (2003) argues that the 'ordinary' people on television are not ordinary like the rest of us; what they possess is the capacity to perform a particularly spectacular version of ordinariness in public. Further, most of the audiences for reality TV would agree that it would be unwise to assume a direct correlation between the identity performed on reality TV and the 'real' identity of the person concerned; indeed, one of the modes of consumption that more avid viewers would report involves the process of carefully watching the performers for the 'authentic' moment when that 'real' self becomes briefly visible (Roscoe, 2001a).

Many of the respondents to research projects such as those conducted by Annette Hill and Bev Skeggs express their distaste for the kind of person they see populating these television shows. In general, they characterize them as celebrity 'wannabes', looking for a shortcut to stardom because they lack the talent to take more conventional routes. That said, there are also plenty of other viewers who applaud precisely that dimension of the format because of the unpredictable outcomes that occur: where the ordinary person, without any particular talent or expectations, emerges, against all the probabilities, triumphant, validated and empowered. At times, it is even possible to laud this as an achievement of some social significance: the winner of the 2004 Australian *Big Brother* was the only black housemate, a Torres Strait Islander called Trevor, an outcome that nobody could have predicted and that a great many welcomed. Overall, even while acknowledging how highly mediated these processes are, it is undeniable that television is now providing more space for the ordinary person to perform a version of themselves than ever before. What is more, some of those who take this opportunity do talk about it as providing them with a form of personal validation and an avenue for self-expression that they describe as empowering.

It is, however, and as I have noted earlier, taking it a step too far to regard the demotic dimensions of reality television as, inherently and consequently, a form of democratization (Dovey, 2000). It is important to recognize that there is a longstanding context for this kind of claim, which has to do with its roots in public interest concerns about the structural imbalance between the power of the media and that of the audience. In this most recent articulation of that debate, reality TV becomes the standard-bearer for an audience-centred critique of the mass media that expresses dissatisfaction with the community's comparative powerlessness to influence directly the character and content of the mass-marketed media products they consume. Broadcast television is here placed among the villains: producing programmes where the audience has no input, with which they may feel little connection, scheduled only at those times that will suit the advertisers, and to which there is often little alternative. As has also been the case with the alternative models represented by user-generated content online, reality TV formats have been very successful in identifying themselves with a populist politics of media consumption. Here, they claim, the interests of the audience have been recovered and the overwhelming power of the producer has been reduced:

> [T]he notion that collective participation in the creation of cultural commodities salvages their claim to authenticity implicitly invokes a critique of the top-down forms of control associated with the culture industry. The corollary of the claim that mass culture is somehow inauthentic because it is created *for* audiences and not *by* them – that, in short, they are in some sense alienated from the production process itself – is that including their participation might help cultural productions reclaim an element of authenticity. In short, that mass culture might regain an element of what media critics Alan O'Connor and John Downing describe as popular culture (as in the sense of 'the people's culture'): forms of entertainment created by and for the people that help typify 'the essence of a people's way of life'. (Andrejevic, 2004: 12–13)

Crucially, this is one of the theoretical contexts into which reality TV has been inserted within media and cultural studies. John Hartley invokes it implicitly when he talks about how the public became 'the star of reality TV formats from *Popstars/Idol* to *Big Brother*':

> Audience interaction was central to such formats, and extended to non-TV platforms including the internet, telephone, and SMS. Successful broadcast shows like *Dawson's Creek* began to introduce interactive elements on the web, such as Sony's 'Dawson's Desk' and 'Rachel's Room' sites, encouraging audiences literally to write themselves into the narrative. (2008: 114)

Such activity is part of the trend towards what Hartley calls 'democratainment' (1999: Chapters 12 and 14; see also Hartley, 2008: 122–4) – literally, the democratization of entertainment. This has been an influential formulation. Versions or adaptations of this idea have become relatively standard features of media and cultural studies accounts of contemporary television over the last decade. As I have noted elsewhere (Turner, 2006) and earlier in this book, while I am persuaded by much of Hartley's argument about the pedagogic function of television, I am not persuaded by the wholesale attribution of a democratic politics to such instances of the demotic turn as reality TV.

I have explained some of my reasons for this position in the previous chapter but there is an additional point I want to make here. The 'democratainment' neologism has to be metaphoric at best. To use the term in a more definitional way over-estimates the power available even to this newly empowered, or Hay and Oullette's 'self-governing' (2008) citizen. Democracy is not so much based upon the mere fact of enfranchisement as upon the power that this delivers to the enfranchised citizen. That is, the entitlement is not the only issue; there is more to democracy than the mere 'aggregation of preferences' (Hindman, 2009: 7). Rather, the citizen's meaningful participation in decision making – which involves the exercise of some form of structural power – is what underpins democracy. I don't accept that the power exercised by audiences in their reading of a text, or by contestants through their participation in a production, is of this order. Nor can these forms of participation be accurately described as a principled system of deliberate choices in the way an explicitly democratic activity might be. To make a crude distinction in order to clarify the point, there is a great deal of difference between the kinds of political power available to the members of Le Bon's unruly crowd, and that available to those voting in their electorate. The power available to the citizen-consumer seems to be closer, most of the time, to that exercised by the crowd than through the electorate. Further, it is clear that some of those who make the strongest claims for democratization are most fundamentally concerned with establishing that the participation they wish to recognize and applaud does have a political dimension. It is certainly possible to accept that claim, and I do, without agreeing that this political dimension is always, or necessarily, of a democratic character.

Furthermore, there are other perspectives from which it is perfectly possible to question the assumption of empowerment as itself an overly optimistic reading of the actual transactions involved. As we have seen, and in what is perhaps the most critical account of reality TV's political potential to emerge from cultural studies' analyses, Mark Andrejevic defines the participation of the ordinary contestant on reality TV as a mode of labour, rather than as the exploration of a new mode of citizenship. That is, he focuses on the contribution that the labour of the participant makes to the creation of value for the producers of a programme; this, rather than focusing on what the contestants might think they are doing for themselves. It is certainly easier to demonstrate the former outcome than the latter. Investigating the kinds of ambiguities and tensions I examined above while teasing out the politics of choice involved in the role of the reality TV contestant, Andrejevic describes the claims of empowerment as a misrecognition of what has actually occurred. As he explains it, these ordinary people's participation in 'the rationalization of their own consumption is sold' to them 'as empowerment' and they have accepted this wholeheartedly (2004: 15). Hence, the close alignment between the comments made by the producers and the participants on this issue. Remarkably, and as we have noted already from the evidence Andrejevic cites, the contestants' claim to personal empowerment appears to be in no way compromised by their subjection to comprehensive regimes of monitoring and surveillance. Indeed, rather than these regimes being regarded as forms of containment that limit the freedom of the individual in order to capture their representation, the contestants that Andrejevic talked to, as well as the producers of the programmes involved, depicted the contestants' submission to comprehensive forms of monitoring and to these programmes' regime of representation as a 'form of empowerment and self-expression' which enables them to be seen and valued for 'just being themselves' (ibid: 14).

Big Brother certainly changed his meaning dramatically as he has made the long journey from Orwell to Endemol: from operating as the dehumanizing voice of totalitarian rule, he has now become the enabling condition for the self-expression of the ordinary person through the mass media.

Constructing cultural identities

In Chapter 1, I referred to the industrialized production of reality TV celebrities as one of the examples of the 'expanded role of a comprehensively commercialised media in constructing cultural identities through new, often participatory and interactive, forms of entertainment across a range of media platforms and formats'. What I want to discuss in this section is the kinds of identities that are produced in such a way.

Earlier, I noted that John Hartley's work has become the classic location for what is a highly positive argument about television's production of cultural identities:

> Television teaches cultural citizenship, and this builds on and extends the civic citizenship of the Enlightenment, the political citizenship of the French Revolution and the social citizenship of industrialization into new rights, namely rights of identity. (Hartley, 1999: 178)

Now, Hartley argues, 'we are moving rapidly past "identity" politics towards something new: citizenship based not an authenticist notion of cultural identity, but on a rapidly decontextualized network of meanings which locate identity in the media sphere, not the public sphere' (1999: 179). This new form of identity he calls do-it-yourself or DIY identity.

Notwithstanding Hartley's marshalling of evidence which demonstrates the potential for personal empowerment through this media-based DIY citizenship, however, it is important to acknowledge that the design options for the DIY process are in fact highly constrained by the limited repertoires of those identities made available to the cultural citizen. This is true both of the public sphere and of this particular DIY media sphere which he addresses. Andrejevic's interviews with the cast members of *Road Rules* reveal the producers' preference for participants who regard their subjective attitude to self-disclosure as a 'form of being honest to oneself and others'. The kind of identity that is 'valorized in such a program', Andrejevic says, can only be achieved through 'full disclosure'. As a result, he quotes numerous expressions of that principle from his interviewees: 'I think I got chosen ... because I kind of just wear my heart on my sleeve'; 'I don't have any skeletons, and I'm a real honest kind'; 'I'm very open with everything, whatever I've done in my life ...'. The producer sums it up: 'We try to cast people who have a natural openness' (Andrejevic, 2004: 106). This is generally the case across reality formats. All the evidence from the screening of the successful audition tapes, usually employed as a means of introducing contestants to the audience in the opening episodes, indicates a clear pattern in the kind of self-presentation preferred. Without exception, contestants are 'outgoing', 'fun-loving', 'extroverts', 'open', 'happy-go-lucky', 'up-for-it', 'risk-takers', 'party-girls/boys' – all guaranteeing the viewer a lively time ahead as we watch their daily lives on screen. It is a very specific kind of lively time, as well, with the promise of self-exposure and excess reinforcing both the voyeuristic expectations and the subcultural identities brought to these programmes by their core viewers.

The difficulty of working through ways of understanding the construction of cultural identities through television is to some extent exacerbated by the complicated and highly conflicting networks of theoretical debate that have developed around it. There are large areas of disagreement in this literature and these have lasted many decades. What has been helpful recently is the emerging availability of some strong, well-theorized and empirical research which has investigated the key issues by talking to audiences and, less often, to producers. The Skeggs and Wood project (Skeggs, 2005; Skeggs and Wood, 2007), as well as the recent book by Annette Hill (2008) I have been referring to throughout this chapter, both have an important empirical dimension and thus provide useful evidence to place against the more exclusively theoretical conjectures about the cultural influence of this format in television and cultural studies over recent years.[9]

In her examination of the contemporary 'making' of class and gender in popular culture, Skeggs (2005) has turned to reality TV (sometimes through what seems to be a synonym, 'cheap television') as a key location where these processes might be examined. She suggests that we are inhabiting a period of what Jon Dovey in *Freakshow* (2000) identified as 'extraordinary subjectivity': 'a shift from grand narratives as the basis for truth claims to statements that the world no longer has purchase unless grounded in the personal, the subjective and the particular' (ibid: 4). This is the world of 'compulsory individuality' (Skeggs, 2005: 973–4). In response to this formulation, Skeggs notes an increasing pervasiveness of grammars of conduct and styles of judgment 'across the practices of everyday life, especially across the media'. The significance of these, she says, is that they are used to organize 'ethical scenarios with maxims and techniques of self-conduct, offering not singular versions of personhood, [but] rather, a plurality of forms of selfhood' that are offered as 'solutions to the dilemmas of existence' (ibid: 973). Faced with this plurality of possibilities, it is up to the individual to 'choose' their repertoire of the self.

This might look like Hartley's DIY citizenship. The problem is that many of our citizens have limited resources to do this: in particular, those elements of the working class who have learned to 'tell' their identities in 'highly specific' but relatively inflexible ways and are thus unable to display themselves correctly in these new ethical scenarios. What they display instead, argues Skeggs (citing the earlier work of Sedgwick, Frank and Valverde), are 'diseases of the will – failures of responsible self control by those who do not know how to behave' (ibid: 974). As a result, Skeggs goes on to suggest that the demotic representatives appearing on reality TV talk shows are there to 'display "bad selves" – those who do not know how to tell [their identities] properly and show that they cannot operate an ethical self':

> These are subjectivities that are out of control, beyond propriety, excessive. They cannot accrue values to themselves because their displays devalue, visually calibrating the failures of self-responsibility. They provide a spectacle of subjectivity turned sour, an epidemic of the will, their own responsibility for making bad choices. (ibid: 974)

Caught within the imperative for taking on compulsory individuality but having little capacity to do so, these subjectivities are poorly performed. Without the access to the resources of the middle class, says Skeggs, 'all they can display is "lack": lack of access to the techniques of telling themselves and lack of access to the right culture; they cannot perform the good self because they do not have the cultural resources to do so' (ibid: 974).

Skeggs's (2005) account suggests that the bad self is always the working-class (and often female) self – the bad parent (*Supernanny*), the bad wife (*Wife Swap*), the bad dresser (*What Not to Wear*). Such programmes recommend models of better selves for emulation: to become better women or men by taking on other modes of behaviour, by acquiring new forms of civility, and so on. However, we also know that popular culture is rarely unequivocally respectful of the norms of civility. Andrew Ross's (1989) account of American intellectuals' relation to popular culture, *No Respect*, and Jane Shattuc's (1998) work on American television talk shows, are just two locations where the contradictory positioning of popular media cultures has been explored. It is a fundamental feature of the traditions of a demotic popular culture that it has the capacity to produce both progressive and reactionary formations at the same time (Dovey, 2000: 116). Indeed, that is very much the situation that Skeggs goes on to describe. Those whose behaviours are offered up as examples of the bad self in these formats and who wish to acquire a better self are also, at the same time, inclined to 'fight back' against that representation (Skeggs, 2005: 975–6). Fighting back involves developing an attack on the pretensions embedded in the 'good' subjectivities of the middle class, and, further, a repudiation of the framework of judgment within which these subjectivities are valued. The result is the shamelessly disrespectful and trashy cultural identities on display in *Big Brother*, *Wife Swap*, *Simple Life* or *The Osbournes*. Not only are these bad selves unrepentantly performed on these shows but the manner of their representation deliberately foregrounds particular tactics of identity maintenance – aggressiveness, competitiveness, selfishness or sexual manipulation, for instance – which are displayed for audience disapproval while at the same time being enjoyed as entertaining performances of demotic excess.

What happens in these programmes is multi-layered and open to quite opposing reading formations. On one level, they present a critique of those who fail to perform appropriately, for instance, while on another level they seem to repudiate the standards against which such failure might be judged. Thus a programme can be explicitly recommending pro-social, civil, middle-class behaviour, while at the same time implicitly exploiting the entertainment value of the performance of the abject or incompetent subjectivity they have used as a means of demonstrating the problems with such unreconstructed behaviour. The pleasures of the entertainment generated by the representation of this undesirable behaviour have the capacity to undermine the implied system of judgment which is used to organize the narrative (but not necessarily the pleasures) of the format. What can happen then – and clearly does so often – is the valorization or even celebration of precisely those behaviours or identities that are excessive, grotesque, offensive or out of control.

To give one example of what I mean here, while no-one could regard Ozzy Osbourne of *The Osbournes* as a model parent, his personal excesses and idiosyncrasies are given enough of a sufficiently sympathetic representation to generate a tolerant and even affectionate response from fans of the show that ultimately celebrates Ozzy's revealed incompetence as an expression of his individuality. This celebration carries very little penalty for the audience. The wider effects of Ozzy's incompetence are significantly neutralized by the equally personalized and celebrated competence of his wife, Sharon. Therefore, it is important to remember that while *Wife Swap*, for instance, might be offering some viewers an opportunity to consider how to become a better self, it might also be offering others the pleasure of watching a deliberately offensive and shameless performance of the demotic as popular entertainment.

Reality TV programmes pose quite a challenge to an egalitarian commitment to the ordinary as well as to any attribution of a progressive politics to the simple fact of its representation. If Bev Skeggs is right to argue that programmes such as these actually help to 'make' class, then there is every reason why those who are being 'made' into this class should react with a defiant proclamation of what the rest of us will need to accept – the unruly incivility of the demotic – if such a transformation is to be accomplished. If you connect this proclamation with the individual achievements we have talked about before – where not only a level of celebrity or visibility is gained but also where there are moments of public validation and social and personal transcendence (I am thinking of formats like *Idol* here but this could also be seen in makeover shows such as *How to Look Good Naked* or *Queer Eye for the Straight Guy* and so on) – then you will have quite a powerful demonstration of just why these programmes might be regarded as serving some kind of socially ameliorative function even as they recycle regressive and trashy representations of working-class cultural identities.

Given all of this, and while it is unwise to accept without question the concerns raised by the moral and media panics around the behaviour of the mass media, it is not surprising that many have tried to argue that reality TV carries with it significant social and cultural effects – for good and for ill – or, the more critical argument, that its preferred identities have colonized the expectations of everyday life in contemporary western societies. In media, communications and cultural studies research, years of failed effects studies have proved that we don't really have the capacity to demonstrate such social effects convincingly. Even if we might agree that there was good reason to examine reality TV's projected effect on the construction of cultural identity, particularly among young people, it is very difficult to isolate the influence of these programmes or of television itself in order to do so. We know the dangers of sliding into a reflectionist view of media influence that simply connects the prevalence of narcissistic identities represented in the media with the possibility that there is an increase in these identities within the community at large. Media and cultural studies have vigorously resisted that kind of argument – in relation to screen violence, for instance – for many years. In general, most of us would agree that is not possible to argue convincingly that the consumption of reality TV necessarily engenders some kind of transfer between a programme and the public that would exercise a determining role on the identities that public might choose or, perhaps, even on the repertoire of identities from which they might choose. The imputed determination doesn't survive even the most basic investigation: for every research project which finds that children are nominating fame as a career goal and *Big Brother* as the preferred route towards that goal, there is another which reports on an audience that is scathing in its assessment of celebrity wannabes and their quest for their moment of fame.

Yet the influence may be less than a determining one and still be worth examining. Where there is some compelling evidence, and where I think there is a strong case for further research, is the generational and gender inflections of this process of identity formation. My opinion, and it is only that, is that within particular class fractions of young people, the cultural identities celebrated within reality TV may have significant purchase, and may well offer themselves up as objects of desire and emulation. Later on in this chapter, we will return to a discussion of aspects of that possibility.

That such a possibility exists at all, then, is worth considering – particularly because these identities are produced and circulated in such a random and perhaps even irresponsible manner. Annette Hill picks up on this when she describes reality TV as a 'feral' genre:

> It is wildly opportunistic in its desire to attract popular viewers around the world; it is de-territorial in its ability to cross generic boundaries; it is disruptive in the production and scheduling of existing factual genres; and, above all, it is resistant to containment. (2008: 215)

Some of these attributes may well be a reason for concern. If the promotion and circulation of programmes such as *Big Brother, Idol, Real World, I'm a Celebrity Get Me Out of Here!* affect the desire for particular formations of cultural identities among young people, perhaps this constitutes the social consequences that are the incidental by-products of the need to create a market for an entertainment programme. These formats claim to provide us with unmediated presentations of 'everyday' life and to set in place enabling structures for individual participants that will definitely affect their everyday lives thereafter. Those who enjoy watching reality TV, and those who don't, actually offer similar accounts of its provenance – even though they will each take quite opposing views on how to respond to this. Both sectors of the audience, for different reasons, take the view that reality TV raises questions about how we think about our lives, about the norms which govern them, and the possibilities they offer.

These are issues on which public and academic opinion in western nation-states remains divided. For every person who would regard reality TV as exercising an unhealthy influence on the behaviour of contemporary youth, there is another who would contest this as a conservative or elitist view of popular culture. However, whatever reservations we might have about how we demonstrate that reality TV actually has a cultural function beyond the entertainment industry, these don't seem to be bothering either the public or the authorities so much outside the West. The audience appeal of western popular culture has always been regarded as a serious challenge to the local culture within nation-states that wish to maintain a distinction between their values and those of the West – for political, cultural, religious or other reasons. In such contexts, the grassroots appeal of reality TV – and, crucially, its claim to represent reality for that audience – suggests that it could be an especially powerful western influence, particularly as it appeals to its audiences over the heads, as it were, of the established systems of political authority and cultural control. Indeed, it is part of the appeal of the reality TV format that, notwithstanding its dependence on monitoring and surveillance, it promises its audience that it will provoke and defy authority.

Many nation-states, in Asia and the Middle East in particular, have decided that this is an important cultural phenomenon to understand and control. The valorization of youth and the excessively self-presentational modes of behaviour recommended to them through the big international formats such as *Idol* are of particular concern to those cultures which maintain a strict cultural tradition of respect for authority and an ethic of self-discipline rather than self-disclosure. In the following section, I want to discuss some instances where western reality TV formats have run up against local cultural norms and values, and where there seems to be no doubt, among those required to regulate the media industries in these instances, about the likely cultural impact of such programmes – that is, of television's potential to challenge and even change social norms and values if it is allowed to remain uncontested or, in some cases, uncensored. While the preceding discussion has really been making the point that western media and cultural studies has to admit that we are ultimately reluctant to form definitive conclusions about the socio-cultural effects of a single television programme or even a collection of formats within our own cultures, those outside the West who regard reality TV as a Trojan horse for western values are not nearly so constrained.

Translating cultural identities

In recent years, the pedagogic potential of television has perhaps been more vigorously exploited by nation-states outside the West than within it. Abu-Lughod's (2005) account of the consumption of television in Egypt, for instance, describes a deployment of the medium which is focused on teaching its viewers how to be citizens of their nation-state. However, even in states where this kind of strategy has been systematically employed, the demotic turn can produce outcomes which will frustrate official plans. In China, the take-up of international formats which was kick-started by the notorious *Supergirl* contest has raised significant issues about the representation of national cultural identity, not only for the government regulators but also for television producers (Keane et al., 2007). The winner of the *Supergirl* contest did not meet the conventional criteria for a Chinese heroine: she was an androgynous tomboy whose success was popularly applauded but who nonetheless demonstrated the potential of commercial transnational entertainment formats to contribute to Chinese popular culture in unsettling ways (Yue and Yu, 2008). Produced by an upstart regional broadcaster, *Supergirl* had, in a sense, slipped through the net which normally ensured that imported and adapted cultural products were strongly marked by 'Chinese characteristics':

> The phrase 'with Chinese characteristics' has become a way of asserting sovereignty in an era that has seen an unprecedented influx of global products, theories and ideologies. Hence, 'Chinese characteristics' not only celebrates adaptation, but more importantly, its application becomes a normative strategy to ensure economic reforms do not become automatically associated with an ideological drift towards liberal governance and celebrations of a consumer society. (Keane et al., 2007: 50)

The official response from the Chinese regulators was to exert pressure on the television producers to modify their transnational formats. This has involved more than the standard 'glocalization' of a transnational, already hybridized, format like *Big Brother* or *Idol*. There is a new, and more urgent, dimension to what have become relatively familiar debates in the West about the homogenization of culture. That is, rather than tailoring a product's entertainment values or popular appeal for an indigenous commercial market (Moran, 2009) in the way we might normally associate with glocalization, we are seeing the modification of the specific content of the cultural identities on offer in these programmes – sometimes actually to the detriment of their entertainment value – for what are overwhelmingly political reasons.

Anthony Fung has written about the modifications made to formats such as *Survivor* and *Who Wants to be a Millionaire?* to bring them into line with the value systems required of television in mainland China (2009). In the Chinese version of *Who Wants to be a Millionaire?*, for instance (called *Happy Dictionary*), cash rewards were first capped and then replaced with useful household consumable items; the western staple of entertainment or celebrity gossip-based quiz questions were replaced with those that drew upon more formal educational knowledge; and rules were introduced to reduce the possibility that all the prizes on offer might fall into the hands of a single individual.

Most importantly, though, it is the individualist and competitive cultural identities that are thoroughly embedded in the structure of the tasks and in the arc of the narrative of a show such as *Survivor* that required modification to support identities consistent with those supported by the Chinese state.[10] There have been a number of versions of this format in which the 'survival of the fittest' engine used to drive the narrative in the western version has been significantly modified to insert 'political messages to do with nationalism, patriotism, [national] unity and multiculturalism' (Fung, 2009: 185). Fung's description of the modifications to a programme called *I Shouldn't Be Alive*, one of several adaptations of *Survivor*, gives some idea of the changes involved:

> [Here] the original focus on egotistic competition and individual belligerence was translated into a 'human versus nature' competition in which participants toured around the 40,000-kilometre-long border of the country over seven months. The local production deliberately diluted the dark side of humanity – the personal conceit, egoism and selfishness that characterized the American version. It cancelled the voting session, used in the original show [*Survivor*] to kick out 'the weak', and expunged shots that might provoke the issue of privacy, emphasizing the hardship and determination of the comrades in arms as they overcame obstacles along the journey. (ibid: 185)

In its second series, *I Shouldn't be Alive: Walking the Long March Road*, the political provenance of the primary task was made explicit as the 20 contestants walked the famous 6,000-kilometre path taken by the Red Army in exile. Fung comments that while it might seem absurd that the producers should attempt to 'insert first a nationalistic ideology and second a social philosophy into a commercial formula', 'it did have a strong appeal in the Chinese context'. As he points out, in contemporary Chinese media, the combination of soft nationalism and commercial entertainment is not uncommon (ibid: 186).

These modifications have avoided the kinds of cultural dissonance so widely attributed to *Supergirl*. There are many other examples, however, of the unforeseen success of globalized western television formats generating widespread public and political concern. One such instance is the adaptation of the UK format *Fame Academy*, renamed *Akademi Fantasia* and produced for Malaysian audiences by Malaysia's sole pay TV provider Astro.[11] *Akademi Fantasia*, like its western model, is a blend of features found in the *Big Brother* and *Idol* formats. One component is a series of weekly concerts in which contestants compete both for the audience vote and for the judges' approval. A second component was initially a weekly talk show in which contestants reflected on their experiences in the academy; this has been replaced in more recent series by a debate involving four panellists discussing some issue related to the academy. The third component involves 'reality' footage which is presented as a diary of the contestants living and working together while they are trained and prepared for their performances. The diary is screened daily and has almost none of the voyeuristic dimensions of the western formats: males and females are housed separately, there are no cameras in areas where privacy may be intruded upon, such as the bathroom, and there is no focus on sexual relations between the contestants as a privileged source of narrative interest or dramatic tension.

By western standards for the content of reality TV, then, *Akademi Fantasia* is a relatively tame affair. Nonetheless, the concerts themselves are very much in the mould of those used in the original format – performed live to large and noisy audiences dressed in the fashions of western youth cultures (with some local modifications), and displaying large placards or signs to signify their support for particular performers. The programme is colourful, frenetic and driven along by an excitable host. The production design foregrounds the gleaming high-tech modernity typical of

twenty-first-century Asia. The overall effect of the concert programmes is slightly chaotic, much in the way of the western
versions, perhaps in order to maintain the prominence of the live
audience's participation as visible surrogates for the virtually co-
present television audience. Popular interest in performing on the
programme has increased dramatically since the first series, so clearly
the target audience desires to inhabit the novel cultural identities on
display. There were 400 applicants for the first season in 2003;
8,000 for the second season; and for season five the programme
makers received seven million applications (Maliki, 2008: 32). It
has, then, become something of a popular culture phenomenon.

Not everyone has been pleased by this. Newspaper reports and
comments from political parties and religious and community
groups found much to criticize in the programme. Malaysia is offi-
cially an Islamic state, and some of the behaviour expected of the
contestants in *Akademi Fantasia* violates Islamic principles. The
New Straits Times reported that members of the governing party
had responded to the show by calling for more stringent controls on
reality TV programmes, and the Deputy Premier issued a statement
in which he warned that these could 'threaten Eastern values and lead
to moral decadence' (ibid: 89). According to Maliki, even moderate Islamists were offended by central aspects of the programme,
expressing concern about its effect on the nation's youth, and calling for a more rigorous government oversight of imported formats.

It is as well to consider what is being protected here. Holding
together the various ethnicities and cultures of Malaysia has been
that country's explicit political objective since a major riot in
1969 which highlighted the necessity of developing a strong political base for a unified national culture. Since that time, substantial
government structures have been put in place to manage and
direct this ongoing process. In some countries, the category of
'national values' might be one which gets filled up with a range of
different kinds of discursive content at various conjunctures,
depending on the strategic or political considerations in play at the
time. That is not the case in Malaysia. One of the strategies used to
create the Malaysian polity was the promulgation of an explicit set
of values declared fundamental to a tolerant Islamic society and
ultimately necessary to ensure good governance (ibid: 82–3). There
can be scant debate about whether a particular television programme

is, or is not, supportive of Malaysian national values. Furthermore, there is little doubt that the government requires television to accept the responsibility of reinforcing those values; television in Malaysia has an explicit legislative mandate to promote national unity (ibid: 84). As is the case with many other nation-states in Asia, there is considerable sensitivity in Malaysia about external threats to their cultural identity and in particular about the need to resist what is regarded as the negative influence of western materialist culture. Legislation decrees that no advertising on local television can glorify western cultures, government regulation is in place to monitor imported programmes so that 'western negative values' are not circulated, and there is an active regime of state censorship.

Consequently, it would not have been surprising if the Malaysian government had decided to ban this programme altogether. There were certainly many calls for this to happen. Aspects of the format and of the behaviour required of the contestants transgressed the norms of a moderate Islam as well as the national values of Malaysia. The cohabitation of the sexes without marriage – even when located in segregated and locked dormitories as in this case – is seen as immoral; the public expression of affection – hugging, kissing, touching a member of the opposite sex, even when that person is your marriage partner – is similarly unacceptable. An excessive public expression of emotion – of the kind that is elicited when a contestant is voted out, for instance – is viewed as shameful. The kind of sexual display routinely expected ˙of female contestants in programmes like *Idol*, and which also occurred in *Akademi Fantasia*, attracted moral condemnation in a society where many women choose to observe Islamic dress codes. More fundamentally, the whole reality TV enterprise itself (the offer of a fantasy of stardom in place of a more realistic, and in a national sense more productive, set of career objectives) was criticized as likely to corrupt the young by feeding them fantasies of material success, thereby rendering them unproductive as members of society (ibid: 93–107). Furthermore, the focus on material goods, the trappings of celebrity, the importance of the individual rather than the community, and material consumption being offered as a key signifier of personal success – all of these run counter to the principles and philosophy of the Islamic state. Reading the press reports, the columns, and the blogs cited in Maliki's discussion, one gains the sense of a society that was alarmed at suddenly finding that this television programme, a mere entertainment, albeit avidly consumed by the nation's young people, seemed to be undoing what generations of disciplined political control had worked hard to achieve. On the other hand, it is also likely that alternative points of view, those which have insisted on Malaysia's need to continue to open itself up to the globalizing, modernizing – even democratizing – influence that is identified with these international television formats, may have contributed to the authorities' eventual decision to register their concerns but to tolerate the programme's continued existence within a slightly modified regulatory context.

Now it would be easy to regard this controversy simply as evidence of global television facilitating the empowerment of its audience to challenge the authority of 'Malaysian values', and thus as a sign of the inevitability of modernization and even democratization in the era of a transnational trade in entertainment products. It is not uncommon for resistance to western influences to be automatically regarded, by those in the West, as simply reactionary, while the prospering of western influences in the face of such resistance is held to constitute a necessary process of political liberalization or to stand as evidence of the cultural benefits of cosmopolitanism. It is probably fair to suggest that many western media scholars would regard the situation that Maliki's research examines, notwithstanding its temporarily divisive effect within the nation-state concerned, as progress: namely, as unlikely in the long term to do any harm to the society concerned other than to nudge it gently towards the globalizing norms framing the modernity of the twenty-first century.

Yet considering the range of concerns quoted in Maliki's research, as well as her own attempt to come to terms with the cultural incompatibilities she is describing, must give some pause to this response. One of the contradictions at the heart of the western desire called cosmopolitanism is, on the one hand, its determination to embrace all cultures as if they are all equally assimilable and, on the other, the tendency for that embrace to overlook the specific cultural sensitivities of those who might be resisting their enclosure within it (Calhoun, 2007: 20–3). It is a paradox, but nonetheless true, that cultural identity, seen from the perspective of the cosmopolitan, can be regarded as expendable if it stands in the way of cosmopolitanism's particular version of modernity.

The difficulty in dealing with this can perhaps be seen in Maliki's research task: attempting to deal with this controversy as an example of media globalization upon which western media theory is the authoritative research source, while also, as a Malaysian Muslim, being embedded in the cultural and religious debates at the heart of the controversy[12] and thus concerned by the cultural and political instability they generate. This plays out in curious ways: for instance, while western media theory warns her against the inadequacy of simple attributions of media effects, her account of the public reception of *Akademi Fantasia* has to acknowledge that this reception (from both the positive and the negative side) takes as a given that what is being observed is the socio-cultural effect of that television programme. In many ways, approaching the controversy from within Malaysia as it does, Maliki's research provokes fundamental questions about how such a nation-state might go about managing its cultural maintenance under these conditions. On the other hand, while the social benefits of the state's management of Malaysian values are not inconsiderable, we know that these have been accomplished through an authoritarian political structure. Maliki's account not only reminds us of the point of such values, however, but it also responds enthusiastically to the attractions of the programme seen so effectively to challenge them. Taking all of these conflicting points of view seriously, one can't help but suspect, nonetheless, that to disregard the local perspective in order to cheerily describe the commercial success of this programme as evidence of modernization, globalization or democratization may well constitute a form of peculiarly western cultural arrogance, blind to the significance of the complex of cultural politics actually in play within that nation-state.

Of course, I am perfectly aware of the dangers of sentimentalizing such a position and I have no interest in mounting a defence of an Islamist Malaysia as a national formation to be preserved in perpetuity, nor of the methods used to manage its construction of national unity. There are a couple of points I want to take from this example, however. The first is that while there is not much consensus (although there is certainly much interest) within western media and cultural studies about the precise extent and effectivity of the influence of popular cultural forms on the personal development of cultural identities, these examples from Asia reflect no doubt at all that the effective leading edge of western values and cultural identities is their media representation.

The second point follows on from the first by asking what might be the consequence if we provisionally accepted the Asian assumptions as legitimate: that is, to accept that the cultural values and identities on display in these formats do have the capacity to produce cultural change in these non-western societies. If this was actually the case, then what I would want to highlight next is the striking disproportion between the relatively short-term objectives of the entertainment product on the one hand and the long-term significance of the projected cultural effect on the other. This asymmetry serves to emphasize how single-mindedly commercial on the one hand, and how ideologically casual on the other, is the trade in cultural identities through global television formats such as *Fame Academy*. As we have seen, understanding how these programmes may exert their influence on how we think about our lives in western cultures remains a matter for further research and debate but, at the very least, the gap between their commercial intentions and their possible cultural effects certainly indicates to me that this is a question that should continue to attract attention – not only in terms of a critique of the claimed effects, but also for the opportunistic manner in which these might be produced.

A final example also underlines not only how directly these programmes might engage with the political construction of cultural identities, but also how unpredictable and contingent are the kind of politics within which they can become embedded. Marwan Kraidy's (2009) examination of the development and reception of reality TV formats within Arab television – both within Arab nation-states and through pan-Arab transnational satellite programming – presents us with a demonstration of the direct relation such programmes can have to ongoing debates about cultural identity as well as the range of political communities with which they can engage. Importantly, too, in its discussion of the unlikely partnership between the finances of the religiously repressive Saudi regime, and the creativity of the more secular and westernised

Lebanese producers, it demonstrates the necessary flexibility required of a commercial enterprise that must negotiate the complications of the Arab region. While the story here may not be quite as 'feral' as that which Hill describes elsewhere – there is a notable sense of political commitment behind some of the programmes Kraidy describes – it is probably even more dramatic a demonstration of the scale and significance of the cultural effects that can be generated by an industry that nonetheless sees them as only by-products of, or obstacles to, their primary commercial activity, and thus to be managed as an issue of marketing and public relations rather than integrated into a political or social objective.

Reality TV has played a particularly lively role in Arab societies, as its reception pits competing versions of modernity against each other and as it raises the fundamental question of who gets to control what counts as 'reality' for that society – popular entertainment formats, the state, the clerisy, or, in the case of the Saudis, the royal family? That question has been answered, in some cases, by repressive action. The local version of *Big Brother* was closed down by the state in Bahrain and the pan-Arab *Star Academy* (*Fame Academy*) resulted in the issuing of a *fatwa* by a Saudi juridical council. In Kuwait, legislators forced a minister to resign for allowing *Superstar* (*Idol*) contestants to hold a public concert. The severity of these responses is an indication of just how much might be at stake, and how significant a role reality TV can play, in these internal political and cultural debates. Kraidy describes it this way:

> ... reality TV is a social laboratory where various versions of modernity are elaborated and contested, a courtroom of sorts that hosts modernity's endless trial. During the trial, various ways of being modern emerge, all involving a combination of media and other institutions playing a central role in mediating modernity, a re-fashioning of individual identities and their relationship to society, and a search for historically resonant and culturally meaningful forms of modernity. Filtering out undesirable aspects of Western modernity and nurturing locally attractive facets is a driving force of the Arab television polemics. (2009: 18)

Comparing the two contexts – the pan-Arab and the Malaysian – reveals significant differences in the kind of ground upon which reality TV makes its contribution in each case. As Kraidy demonstrates in fascinating detail throughout his book, there is already – that is, well in advance of the controversy over these programmes – a volatile, longstanding and highly nuanced debate within the Arab context about how precisely to engage with the various versions of modernity, as well as who gets to authorize 'authentic' versions of cultural identity. Whereas the Malaysian situation is one where a level of stability seems to have been established or enforced, which is highly valued as a fundamental socio-political objective by all parties, and where there is little current indication of grassroots activists awaiting the opportunity provided by the reality TV moment,[13] the Arab situation is multiply inflected in each nation-state by what Kraidy calls 'an explosive cocktail of religion, politics, gender and money' that is already highly active and vigorously debated. In this context, the claims made by reality TV to represent reality are a direct provocation to existing cultural formations around identity, gender, religion and modernity; thus an engagement with these claims seems to be unavoidable for all kinds of social and political formations. As far as the nature of these existing cultural formations is concerned, Kraidy is insistent that the objections to *Star Academy* and other hybridized formats should not be seen as 'the battle cry of tradition against modernity' – something that might well be said about the Malaysian debate. Rather, he argues that the Saudi reaction to *Star Academy*, to take one example, is 'symptomatic of a struggle between rival versions of Saudi modernity: the Saudi debate over authenticity reflects a struggle to accommodate change without relinquishing one's identity' (ibid: 117). This is not, of course, a new struggle but could be said to be almost constitutive of the history of the Saudis' relationship with the West.

Kraidy provides examples of how contingent the role of reality TV is, on the one hand, but also how readily it becomes engaged with existing debates about cultural identities of all kinds – national, gendered, religious, and so on – on the other. Consequently, he is also keen to argue against the western assumption that such an engagement will necessarily have a liberal political agenda, and will work towards a liberal end. The notion of democracy has, he says, been irredeemably tainted by its association with the Bush administration in the USA and its attempts to remake the Middle East. In its place, for the moment, is a notion of justice that underpins the defence of the rule of law but which still locates power with the state rather than with the citizen. Kraidy also demonstrates that the role of reality TV in the Arab world is not confined to the marketing of hybridized formats that privilege western forms of entertainment. Several Arab reality TV shows he mentions are directed towards reaffirming local social norms. In a region where poetry plays a prominent public role, we have *Millionaire Poet* and *Prince of Poets* re-enacting traditional poetry contests in the Gulf states to 'reaffirm tradition but within a modern frame' and achieving 'considerable success' (ibid: 209). *Star Academy* has also 'been re-appropriated as a competition in Qur'anic recitation' (ibid: 209).

According to the account presented in Kraidy's book, there seems to be no question about these media formats' implication in important social and cultural debates within the Arab region. The precise nature of that implication, and the politics it engenders, varies dramatically according to the histories with which it intersects. In the contexts Kraidy describes, as in the Malaysian instance Maliki examines, there seems little doubt that these programmes are embedding new versions of cultural identity within the promise of globalized entertainment. It is not surprising, therefore, that although as mere entertainments they may seem abstracted from the political realm, they have played a significant role in these societies' debates about cultural identities, constituting new platforms for 'proxy battles to draw boundaries between reality and the image, the masculine and the feminine, the pure and the hyrid, the authentic and the foreign' (ibid: 15).

Conclusion

If it is true, as I have suggested, that the media have entered a phase in which they now operate as the authors or translators of cultural identities, then reality TV must be right at the forefront of that trend. The performance of cultural identity is its staple component, and the audience's recognition of and engagement with those identities among its primary pleasures. Paradoxically, what makes the performance so powerful and attractive is its integration into a format predicated on dissolving the boundaries between the represented and the real: between TV and real life. While this objective is in one sense a fantasy, to the extent that the format does manage to do this it constitutes an extension of the media's power. Through reality TV the media have managed to reach across those erstwhile boundaries and entwine themselves in the intricacies of everyday life so that we no longer find it quite so easy to separate these modalities out. Then, the media put all of that on television in regular slots, five nights a week, at the same time. Through this representation of the performance of everyday life, and through its patterns of scheduling and access, television reasserts its embeddedness in everyday life.

Given the history of television as a domestic medium, it is not surprising that many in media, cultural and television studies see these programmes as a dramatic extension of the pedagogic capacity of the medium, and thus as an essentially positive force aimed at helping us become better selves through the models for 'better living' (Hay and Oullette, 2008) demonstrated on screen. Even as I see that kind of potential in many examples, I am sceptical about the comprehensive ambitions of such accounts. As one maps the demotic turn in popular culture, one frequently encounters instances where it is explained in terms of political enfranchisement. The rise of the demotic voice on talk radio, the subject of Chapter 4, is one instance where the politics of media access can be read in ways that do not amount to a simple case of enfranchisement. Further, there are many instances where such rationalizations are used for the express purpose of defending activities against accusations of them exploiting, misleading or manipulating their participants. Reality TV producers do this all the time.

There are lots of reasons why we might be inclined to accept such rationalizations. It has to be admitted that there is something inherently seductive about the demotic content we have been describing. Its proximity to the everyday lives of audiences increases their sense of identification with the participants, their affective investment in the narratives and dramas, as well as an audience confidence in their own capacity to engage actively and critically with the texts – to make them over to their own purposes. It would be pleasing to believe that something with which we feel such a close connection was also good for us.

I am not interested, however, in arguing that the demotic turn as it is instantiated in reality TV is a categorically 'good' or 'bad' thing. I would argue that it is powerful. Worryingly, though, that power doesn't seem to need to have a principled base. The demotic in reality TV is unruly, unpredictable, or just 'feral' as Annette Hill calls it. As a result, and particularly for the non-western markets I have referred to, the fact that reality TV also operates so effectively as a translator of cultural identities is potentially disturbing. Among the purposes of translation is to enable consumption and thus to enhance the accessibility of the identities such programmes carry. While it might suit the entertainment industry to argue that their projects are harmless enough, programming which sets out to produce cultural identities as a means of marketing a particular product does carry the capacity to generate significant, if unintended, cultural effects.

The motivation behind the activities which produce these unintended cultural effects, most of the time, is commercial rather than political or cultural. Reality TV formats have been the booming stocks in the global television market over the last decade. While there are some signs of format exhaustion – *Big Brother* and *Idol* are both declining in the markets where they were so successful early on – the price of coming up with new formats is low, the international trade is expanding, and the returns can be very high indeed. There is, then, a strong commercial reason for developing new franchises and new audiences, and for pursuing one more format mutation.

Reality TV, given its close but ambiguous relation to everyday life, has the capacity to be an extraordinarily engaging means of generating a broad-based conversation between audiences, producers and the nation at large. There have been plenty of moments when that has occurred – and not just in the explicitly pro-social examples like *Jamie's School Dinners* but also in the politically dynamic contexts that Marwan Kraidy describes. However, reality TV's demonstrated tendency to resist working consistently within such a frame is to do with commercial imperatives, with the need for reality TV to transform its relatively benign role as cultural scribe or interlocutor into that of the edgy and controversial commercial entertainer in order to meet the market's demand for novelty, colour and excess. As a result, despite the demotic social location of programmes, the actual performance of the demotic over time in most formats is actually quite selective and motivated. That performance trends almost inevitably towards the excessive, the extraordinary and even the offensive as a means of attracting the attention of its audience. And so when we design the coordinates which map the production of the cultural identities through these formats, one axis would have to bear the words 'commercial imperatives' as among the primary determinants of their design.

Notes

1 See Dovey (2000: Chapter 4) for an early overview of these debates.
2 There was, of course, the 2007 racism accusations related to her treatment of a fellow contestant in Celebrity Big Brother, Bollywood star Shilpa Shetty, but she has also been the site of debate between those who see her media treatment as the expression of class prejudice and those who see her celebrity as symptomatic of cultural decline. For an example of how her career has been examined within the academic literature on television and celebrity see Rahman (2008).
3 Subsequently, there was something of a public debate about how the media should treat Goody's public battle with cancer, as her condition worsened and the crassness of such commentary became more apparent. UK commentators on the situation included the Prime Minister, Gordon Brown and Shilpa Shetty. This debate reached its peak when Goody died in 2009.
4 Ross (2009: 136–7) reports that in Mexico, the producers of Kid Nation have been investigated for breaching child labour laws. In the Australian version of Popstars, one of the girls selected to form the first singing group (eventually called Bardot) is reputed to have declined the contract that eventuated because it tied her up for five years. When she was unceremoniously removed from the house in which she and the other singers were living during the 'training' period, a rumour was allowed to circulate throughout the media that suggested her departure was related to the discovery she had been stealing from the other girls.
5 That is, they were not offered opportunities that they saw as career opportunities. They were only used as promotional devices for the series or the network.
6 This refers to the practice of using male genitalia to 'slap' someone's face.

7 Andrejevic has followed up this issue, making the role of surveillance in the interactive era the focus of his (2007) book, *iSpy*.

8 Ironically, it seems that those who can't stand reality TV are foremost among those who relate it to contemporary realities as somehow symptomatic; the paradox here is that they may well be attributing a greater authenticity to it than those who actually enjoy watching it.

9 Throughout this section of the chapter, I am going to be drawing at some length on work that Bev Skeggs and her collaborator Helen Wood have published out of their research project entitled 'Making Class and Self through Televised Ethical Scenarios'. This project has focused upon reality TV and contemporary theories and modes of identity formation, and while it is, I believe, still under way, it has already provided some very useful pointers to issues relevant to my own concerns here.

10 There are other examples of this kind of modification from different contexts. The Lebanese version of *Pop Idol* (*Superstar*) focused on apprenticeship and mentoring rather than humiliation, for instance, while the title of the Arab version of *The Biggest Loser* (*Al-Rabeh al-Akbar*) means 'The Biggest Winner' (Kraidy, 2009: 32).

11 Astro offers over 100 channels with programmes that appeal to a multi-ethnic and multi-lingual audience; it reaches 35.8 per cent of Malaysian homes with televisions (Maliki, 2008: 22).

12 I was Jamilah Maliki's supervisor for the MPhil research project discussed here. It is at this stage unpublished.

13 I should acknowledge that I am no expert on Malaysian politics, so there may be an element of naivety in this comment; however, what I am highlighting is the fact that there is a clear difference between the visibility and prominence of a public politics of transgression within the situation Kraidy describes and that which Maliki describes – even though the role of the state in both contexts is authoritarian and interventionary.

3

Redefining Journalism: citizens, blogs and the rise of opinion

Among the prime casualties of the demotic turn is the professional production of journalism. As newspaper proprietors talk of dwindling prospects for the print media, as television news and current affairs programming continues to morph into entertainment and lifestyle genres, and as news and current affairs on radio is turned over to the populist talk show host, the prospects for traditional journalism look bleak. Ironically, at the same time, the public has never had such a comprehensive and continuous access to news, and new kinds of journalism seem to be emerging every day through online platforms or subscription television. However, the expansion of the supply of news through such avenues has not necessarily opened the door to a journalism which defines itself through a set of explicitly professional practices such as a hierarchical editorial structure, a programme of professional training, a code of ethics or the equivalent, and a principled focus on verifiable news and information.

Instead, and in a further iteration of the situation I referred to in the previous chapter, the key element of the current environment is that, as audiences lose faith (or interest) in the traditional version of the profession's output, and as increasing numbers express their concern about the undesirable concentration of power in the mainstream media industries, the emerging platforms for journalism are drawing on the voices of their publics. These voices can serve many different political and commercial agendas. Their platforms include the various citizen and public journalism projects, the news blog and the proliferating 'alternative' news sites which are just as happy to publish an interesting contribution from an amateur Joe Public as a more conventionally journalistic article from a moonlighting professional.

As a result of these new platforms opening up, and notwithstanding what many regard as a 'crisis' in the profession,[1] there is a great deal of journalism around right now. The problem (and there is, on balance, a problem) is that this does not necessarily mean that the increased volume has made journalism better, more reliable or more diverse in terms of its political perspectives and sources of information. In fact, the reverse seems to be the case. As commercial competition becomes more intense, and as news outlets seek innovative ways to find their audiences, news agendas are narrowing and their content is mutating into hybridized infotainment genres. The merging of news and entertainment, as well as an ongoing industrial integration between the activities of journalism, public relations and publicity, is redefining journalism both for its practitioners and for its audiences. As a consequence, much of what is available to us as news today is produced in a manner which challenges traditional conceptions of the journalist. One aspect of this challenge is that the once privileged position occupied by journalists has been reclaimed, as it were, by those who wish to enable ordinary citizens to participate more directly in the construction of the public sphere. There are certainly plenty of citizens (although as we shall see in Chapter 5, not necessarily 'ordinary') who are interested in taking such an opportunity. Portions of the audience, it seems, no longer want the media to mediate any more; these people now choose to get their news, as they like it, direct from the sources they select – or else they simply choose to make it themselves.

In the online environment, in particular, there are now many alternatives to the professional news organizations; significantly, many of them are quick to point out that they are not run by qualified journalists. Occasionally, in this new environment, the lack of a professional journalism credential or editorial control is actually presented as a positive – a sign of independence or of a direct connection to the community, and thus of a kind of grassroots legitimacy (an example of this is the US site Examiner.com). There are other developments in the western media, also, which explicitly set out to incorporate ordinary citizens into the production of news. We have projects such as 'public journalism' (Glasser, 1999) in local print media, for instance, or the continuing movement in support of the 'citizen journalism' ventures across the media involving what Jay Rosen (2006) calls 'the people formerly known as the audience' in a mixture of professional and amateur (or 'pro-am') capacities. These initiatives have attracted support as a means of responding to what has become a widely held view that the mainstream news media have lost their connection to the community, that they have become too closely affiliated with big business, and that the cultural and social authority once invested in the figure of the independent journalist is no longer justified (Hallin, 1994: 174–80). Popular scepticism about, and even disrespect for, the authority and independence of the journalist has actually been built into some current news media formats – and indeed, as noted in Chapter 1, it could be regarded as being among the motivations behind the shift in news values usually referred to as tabloidization. The development of talk radio in the USA and Australia has radio news and current affairs programmes turned over to the audience, moderated (to use the word loosely) in most cases by a host who is primarily responsible for making a programme entertaining rather than informative, and who depends upon ordinary people phoning in for the content and much of the entertainment. The host establishes their legitimacy in the classic tradition of political populism by privileging the validity of the demotic voice against any other, particularly more institutionalized or elite, forms of authority.

The transformation of news into entertainment has been enabled by, among other things, two apparently contradictory developments. One is the incorporation of the audience into the generation of the content of the news and consequently into its commercial appeal, and the other is the rise of opinion to become virtually the primary genre of content. The political blog is, in many ways, as perfect an example of this as talk radio; the political blog is probably the pre-eminent location where opinion offers itself as information, where consumers' comments constitute a substantial component of the format's content and attraction, and where news is exploited as a means of generating the engagement that is fundamental to the format.

In this chapter, I want to begin by briefly following the narrative of decline I have sketched out here, before examining the extent to which online journalism – through citizen journalism and political or news blogging – might be seen to be correcting the situation as it redefines journalism's relation to its audience and attempts to meet that audience's demands for entertainment, opinion and participation. While talk radio will come up from time to time in this chapter as a key example of some of the shifts I want to outline, a more developed discussion of the various iterations of the talk radio format will be deferred to the following chapter where it is dealt with in detail as one of the key locations for the exploitation of the demotic voice.

The narrative of decline

I have already referred to a liberal critique of the media which sets out to reclaim some access and agency not only for the audience but also for the public at large. Hallin's early warnings about the declining value of journalism within the public sphere described it as 'the passing of high modernism' in American journalism (1994: 170–80), and his book remains an excellent account of the symptoms of this condition, more than a decade since it was first published. According to such a position, the asymmetrical distribution of power, that sees the media in control not only of the flow of information but effectively of the whole of the symbolic economy, is regarded as elitist, anti-democratic and as contributing to the running-down of the public sphere. While this point of view still defends the media's democratic function as the fourth estate, it is extremely critical of how effectively and disinterestedly that role has been played in recent times. Underlying such criticism is the proposition that the legitimacy of the fourth estate has declined as the news industries have operated more and more like conventional commercial businesses. Once it was held as axiomatic – by regulators, politicians, and the public – that the media industries should remain distinct from, unaligned with, and certainly not incorporated within, other realms of commerce or business. Their structural independence was to ensure their political independence for their all-important 'watchdog' role. The submersion of that principle and the mainstream media's subsequent enclosure within the domain of business have given rise to the kinds of critique to which I have been referring.

It is probably important to stress that there is nothing radically new about such a critique; it has been around – and building – for quite some time. As we have seen earlier in this book, criticism of the tabloidization of news draws upon such principles quite heavily. There are, of course, many accounts of that trend and its implications for the production of journalism and for journalism's participation in the public sphere so I am not going to rehearse them in any detail here.[2] The reading lists for journalism courses in the universities are full of such arguments, of course, as academics like myself present their ideas to those going out to seek work in the profession. Indeed, employers often complain about the critical attitudes of new recruits, who want to renovate existing professional practices as soon as they hit the office. The first task for these employers is to acculturate such new recruits to whatever happens to be the case in the newsroom in which they have ended up and so it is understandable if the critical orientation of so much journalism education becomes a little annoying to those charged with that task.

Given that situation, then, it is worth remarking on the extent to which the critique of journalism's thoroughgoing commodification is now turning up within conversations that are *internal* to the profession – in presentations at industry conferences and, most notably, in industry blogs. Among the staple contributions to news blogs and online news sites these days are posts from journalists lamenting the decline of what they regard as valuable – even fundamental – aspects of their profession. Take the following, for example: a sardonic list comparing the rules of 'old school' TV journalism with 'new school' TV journalism, in a blog on 'TV, media and modern life' called *The Feed*, written by a journalist from the *St Petersburg Times* in Tampa, in the United States:

Old rule: news is news. **New rule:** news is marketing.
Old rule: live shots complement the story. **New rule:** live IS the story.
Old rule: staff experience is valuable. **New Rule:** 1 year is experience.
Old rule: weather gets the attention it deserves. **New rule:** rain is a lead story.
Old rule: cover breaking news. **New rule:** make up breaking news.
Old rule: report the facts. **New rule:** report what people say.
Old rule: follow the news director's lead. **New rule:** who's the news director? (Deggans, 2008)

There is more – with numerous comments along the same lines posted in response. This is typical in that it picks up on the commercialization of the practices of journalism while highlighting the loss of what another journalist blogger calls 'the ideal of proportionality', or the matching of the scale and tenor of news coverage against the importance of the story (Harris, 2008). Once, Harris says, 'the elite papers and network news set the agenda, and others followed suit, following up on what these establishment pillars deemed important'. 'Now', he writes, 'it's just the opposite. The conservative voices increasingly take their cues from the new, more daring ones'. The problem with this is as follows:

> Politicians know that as long as they have a base of support they can probably ride out any story confident that the pack will soon move on. Only a news media with the focus and discipline to distinguish a big story from a small one can hold the politicians accountable – and produce the work that deserves an audience. (Harris, 2008)

The effects of this loss of proportionality can be seen not only in the kind of sensationalism customarily targeted in the tabloidization critique but also in a narrowing news agenda. The Pew Center report, 'The State of the News Media 2008', audited news coverage in the USA and found that in 2007 the war in Iraq and the 2008 election campaign occupied more than a quarter of the available space (what is commonly called 'the newshole'). At the same time, a total of less than 1 per cent of the total newshole was devoted to a raft of domestic issues, including education, 'race', religion, transportation, the legal system, drug trafficking, gun control, welfare, social security, ageing, labour and abortion (Project for Excellence in Journalism [PEJ], 2008).

While these developments are usually justified in terms of a need to 'meet the market' – to find new ways to attract audiences or readers – that is clearly not working very well. Network audiences for television news and current affairs programmes have declined dramatically in many western markets; those that I follow most closely (the USA, the UK and Australia) are all experiencing this. (In the United States and Britain, the alarming complication is that the decline is occurring within the context of small but significant increases over 2008 in the total numbers currently watching television.) Readership of newspapers is also declining to the point where newspaper proprietors are openly canvassing the urgent need to develop a new business model that looks to generate significant income from their online platforms. Even though some have been successful at this, and most have been able to boost their total audience numbers if not their revenue through online activities, the effect for US proprietors is still a net loss in readership overall (PEJ, 2008).

In Australia, according to Sally Young (forthcoming), television news and current affairs audiences have declined on average by between 6 per cent and 35 per cent, depending on the programme, over the last seven years (prime-time news bulletins tend to fall into the middle of that range). Television consumption of news and current affairs by the youth demographic (that is, 0–17 years) has dropped by 38 per cent nationally over that same period! The number of newspapers sold per head of the population has almost halved over the last two decades. In the USA all traditional sources of news have declined, and there is also an alarming deficit of news consumption among the young. A worrying 34 per cent of those under 25 consumed no news at all in a typical day. Since the 1990s, the proportion of Americans who say they read a newspaper on a typical day has declined by about 40 per cent; the proportion that watches nightly network news has fallen by a half and now stands at 29 per cent (Pew Research Center, 2008). In the UK, total audiences for television news on terrestrial channels are gradually declining – around 17 per cent over the period 1994–2006 – with the commercial channel, ITV, faring the worst (Ofcom, 2007: 19). In the case of newspapers, despite still enjoying one of the highest levels of newspaper readership in the world, the UK market is in decline – shedding 13.6 per cent of overall sales between 1996 and 2005. The frequency of consumption has also decreased since 2002: those who read a newspaper daily are down from 43 per cent to 36 per cent, and the market leader, *The Sun* (which has accounted for nearly half the total circulation in the popular daily market since 1995), has lost 20 per cent of its circulation over the last decade (ibid: 31–2). In the middle of all this, as these media businesses do their best to negotiate significant commercial obstacles while trying to hang on to their core activities, their audiences regard them as increasingly commercially motivated on the one hand and of diminishing credibility on the other (ibid: 10).

On the positive side, online news consumption has increased in most markets,[3] although this growth is still closely articulated to the web-sites of mainstream media organizations – usually the print or television news media. Most of these are reporting an increase in traffic through their sites, not only for their editorial content but also for their links to other sites or networks. They are, then, becoming service providers as well as stand-alone products or preferred destinations for their audiences/customers. Largely, the proprietors of mainstream news organizations have chosen to develop their online sites for the consumption of entertainment and lifestyle information as well as news – with picture galleries, 'hot' videos, links to entertainment, tourism, consumer information and social neworking sites, and proportionally less 'hard' news than is featured in their print version or television bulletins. The amount of new content on these platforms – that is, content which originates in, or is unique to, a particular site – is relatively small. When Ofcom researchers investigated a major search engine which boasted it could update 4,500 news sources continuously they found that 'virtually all of these apparently diverse "sources" from all around the globe were, in reality, posting the same news stories, using the same words, lifted directly from one or other of four key international sources – Reuters, AP, AFP or the BBC' (ibid: 36). Anyone searching for news stories through a feed such as Google Reader will come up with a similar result as items from 'competing' outlets will be aggregated in a way that reveals they mostly repeat the same headlines and virtually the same stories.

Despite what looks like a massive increase in the supply of news, the real development has not been in the expansion of content: indeed, the insatiable, and unmet, demand for new content has become the primary twenty-first-century problem for contemporary media industries trying to find a way to 'monetize' their participation in multi-platform ventures. Rather, the key change has been the mainstream news sites' translation of news into entertainment. The morphing of news into entertainment online is probably more visible on these sites than it is in their parent organs, but it is a sign of the future – or at least of what the embattled news media of today think is likely to be the future. Nonetheless, this is the platform for which there is a definite upward trend in consumption, and to which the younger demographics who have largely abandoned the print media and broadcast television now seem most likely to transfer their interest and, possibly, loyalty. The positive sign being noted here, and from which the industry is gradually learning its lessons, is that as these online news sites become more closely connected with the growth in social networking sites (through interfaces which enable the sharing of stories, pictures, and so on), the potential for consumers themselves to become producers, freely performing some of the labour required to generate and distribute the content demanded, increases dramatically.

That, as we will see in the next section, carries with it a number of different possible scenarios for journalism and the demotic turn. The access to digital technologies – with the attendant capacity for producing, copying and circulating content cheaply and easily – has given new hope for projects such as public journalism. The public journalism initiative was aimed at connecting journalists in the local print media with their community by making the selecting, gathering and editing of news a collaborative community activity (Glasser, 1999). At the beginning, in the 1980s, this was achieved through a traditional production platform – a hard-copy local newspaper. The shifts in production and consumption that have occurred since then have created the conditions for the next phase of participation which sees the production process also placed in the hands of citizen-contributors. So-called 'citizen journalism' argues that the potentialities of the online environment must be taken up and prosecuted vigorously in order to change the character of news, redistribute the power that resides in those who manage the production of news, and use these new configurations to direct the production of news towards the needs and interests of its consumers. In the following section, I want to examine these possibilities more closely.

'The people formerly known as the audience'

New York University journalism professor Jay Rosen is one of the activists behind the 'citizen journalism' idea, and the author of the formulation quoted in the subheading for this section. His 2006 post to *PressThink* amounts to something of a manifesto for citizen journalism, written in the guise of a letter to 'Big Media' from 'the people formerly known as the audience'. Quoting it at some length is perhaps the quickest way of outlining the argument for, and giving the flavour of the rhetoric attached to, citizen journalism:

> The people formerly known as the audience are those who *were* on the receiving end of a media system that ran one way, in a broadcasting pattern, with high entry fees and a few firms competing to speak very loudly while the rest of the population listened in isolation from one another – and who *today* are not in a situation like that *at all*.

> - Once they were your printing presses; now that humble device, the blog, has given the press to us. That's why blogs have been **called** little First Amendment machines. They extend freedom of the press to more actors.
> - Once it was *your* radio station, broadcasting on *your* frequency. Now that brilliant invention, **podcasting**, gives radio to us. And we have found more uses for it than you did.
> - Shooting, editing and distributing video once belonged to you, Big Media. Only you could afford to reach a TV audience built in your own image. Now video is coming into the user's hands, and audience-building by former members of the audience is alive and well on the Web.
> - You were once (exclusively) the editors of the news, choosing what ran on the front page. Now we can edit our news, and **our choices** send items to our own front pages.
> - A highly centralized media system has connected people 'up' to big social agencies and centers of power but not 'across' to each other. Now the horizontal flow, citizen-to-citizen, is as real and consequential as the vertical one. (Rosen, 2006; emphases in original)

There are limits to citizens' reclamation of power, however; the manifesto makes the point that this is only a shift in power relations, not their complete inversion:

> Look, media people. We are still perfectly content to listen to our radios while driving, sit passively in the dark of the local multiplex, watch TV while motionless and glassy-eyed in bed, and read silently to ourselves as we always have.
>
> Should we attend the theatre, we are unlikely to storm the stage for purposes of putting on our own production. We feel there is nothing wrong with old-style, one-way, top-down media consumption. Big Media pleasures will not be denied us. You provide them, we'll consume them and you have yourselves a nice little business.
>
> But we're not on **your clock** any more. Tom Curley, CEO of the Associated Press, has **explained** this to his people. 'The users are deciding what the point of their engagement will be – what application, what device, what time, what place'. (Rosen, 2006; emphases in original)

Rosen is entitled to claim that there has been a significant shift in media power as a result of the spread of digital technologies. In the case of journalism, the incorporation of amateur or citizen journalism into the regular production of news is a genuine innovation, clearly proving capable of influencing the asymmetry of power referred to earlier on in this chapter. The interactive capacities enabled, and the ease and cheapness with which content can be created for and loaded onto the Web, have significantly affected the cost of production and circulation and expanded the number of those who can afford to be involved (although it is important to remember there are still significant economic and geographic limitations to this involvement). The development of user-friendly, low-cost content management tools such as Movable Type, Blogger.com and Manila has helped facilitate a rapid growth in the number and popularity of independently published web-sites (Thurman, 2008: 140). This growth has been mobilized by a strong idea, the need to renovate the relationship between the media and their audiences, from the grassroots upwards, by starting with the methods used to generate the content in the first place. Citizen journalism aims at reinvigorating the public sphere through the participation of groups of citizens in collecting, reporting, analysing and disseminating news and information online. The level of publicity surrounding citizen journalism as an idea is certainly disproportionate to the number of successful ventures, but the interest in the idea suggests how desirable an alternative it seems. Often embedded in the technological boosterism that usually accompanies the polemics for Web 2.0 and the interactive revolution it is assumed to engender, citizen journalism is clearly an ideal that is enormously attractive to those 'people formerly known as the audience' who want a viable alternative to what they like to call Big Media.

Whether we have this alternative yet, or indeed if we ever will, is another matter. Reports on successful citizen journalism projects are not numerous, and as Flew and Wilson (forthcoming) suggest, the academic literature is 'over-reliant upon a small number of relatively familiar international exemplars, such as the *Indymedia* (Independent Media Centre) network or Korea's *OhMyNews*'. The December 2008 bombings in Mumbai generated international discussion of the potential of citizen journalism as a result of the low levels of information emerging early in that crisis, and the need for news organizations to take up whatever sources they could find (Mishra, 2008). There was some video material circulated by amateurs, and also notable use of the messaging network, Twitter, as a means of circulating information among social networks. The manner in which citizen journalism is organized, however – that is, most often through collectives formed around virtual locations in the West – does not equip it particularly well to take up the slack for the profession when a crisis arises or a disaster happens. Text messaging, or to a lesser extent blogging, seems to be the key communication strategy that takes over at that point. Consequently, the primary story to emerge from the Mumbai bombings, for those interested in the current condition of journalism, was simply the low level of international and national news coverage immediately available (Guthrie, 2008). That a major city of this size and importance should not have an army of foreign correspondents ready to file, in addition to a network of local journalists who might inform them, demonstrated how deeply international news coverage has been cut in recent years. The only international network there was CNN, and only then because they happen to have been assigned to cover another story at the time.

Given the demonstrable failure of citizen journalism to step up to the plate and fill the gap in this situation,[4] it is probably not surprising that there remains a relatively widely held view within the journalism profession, if not within the academy and relevant sections of the public, that the potential of citizen journalism has been 'oversold' (Thurman, 2008: 146); namely, that while its potential is acknowledged, its actual take-up and achieved influence have fallen well short of the predictions made by its more enthusiastic advocates. Similarly, the revolutionary rhetoric often used to make claims for the democratizing influence of weblogs is possibly also responsible for what Thurman describes as a 'subtle distaste for the form', evident in his interviews with mainstream journalists. There is some justification for this, in my view; the rhetoric can be a little excitable (Bruns, 2008b) and short on actual evidence of impact. If you were looking for a notable trend in the contemporary media, for instance, then the widespread disengagement of the youth audience from the consumption of news would be of far greater significance and certainly much easier to demonstrate.

If few people, though, could name a citizen journalism project in their neck of the woods, most would have noticed and possibly even made use of the interactive capacities available to them every day through the mainstream news sites – posting comments about a story in the *Guardian*, for instance, or through the blogosphere, where comments can build into a long-running international conversation. No longer do we have to fume quietly about a story we have read in a newspaper, or fire off a letter to the editor in the (usually vain) hope that it will be published. Now we can often engage directly with the writer, and those who write in support of their point of view. Increasingly, also, the option of writing one's own blog is being explored. Universal McCann research reports 184 million people, worldwide, have taken up this option so far (Technorati, 2008). There is an observable difference between how these issues play out in the various contexts: the commercial online news sites attached to the mainstream media continue to pitch to the mass market – indeed, in many cases it seems as if the online presence is even more commercially oriented than the hard-copy newspaper or the broadcast bulletin. The blogs, however, go for the niches, gathering their own small but loyal audiences and eschewing the temptation to go 'Big'.

It is true, of course, that most of those who choose to interact with the news media do so, overwhelmingly, through these mainstream sites – newspapers such as the *New York Times* or the *Guardian*, television networks such as CNN or the BBC, and so on. Matthew Hindman has pointed out, as well, that online audiences are far more concentrated on the top 20 news sites than newspaper readers are on the top 20 newspapers, so, as he puts it, 'a shift from print to pixels doesn't necessarily promote greater fragmentation' (2008). It is also true that just because news is presented online that does not necessarily mean that it will be more critical, more liberal, or take a more pluralistic approach. This is true of the menu of choices available overall as well as the performances of particular sites. For a start, the way that search engines work is to aggregate content and, consequently, far from providing us with a list of great diversity and plurality, this effect tends to produce a relatively uniform set of results, thus narrowing the news agenda and the range of sources and perspectives easily revealed. There is also a question about the breadth of the news values in operation through online news sites. Research on the media coverage of the 2007 election campaign in Australia compared the election news on 400 television and radio stations with 800 internet news sites and found that 'the differences between the news carried on the Internet and the news published through other media ... were not of a kind that champions of the Internet would have welcomed' (Goot, 2008: 100). The internet turned out to privilege the incumbent government over its opponents (more than was the case for the rest of the media) but, more significantly, to narrow the focus of the news agenda onto the major players and to thus further marginalize the minor parties and independents (ibid.). As Goot says, that is not the kind of consequence one would expect from a multiplication of outlets or from the expansion of the depth and breadth of coverage (that is, the effects of not being constrained by space on the page or time on air) that is presumed to flow from the production logics of the internet.

It should also be stressed that while those boosting the prospects of Web 2.0 and digital technology for transforming journalism have positioned the online news sites and political bloggers as alternatives to the traditional forms and outlets of journalism, there have been a number of studies which highlight the symbiotic character of the relationship between journalists and bloggers. Journalists tend to use blogs as a way of connecting with their audiences (or, as the research in question puts it, 'measure sentiment') and checking up on the competition, rather than as a research tool or as an alternative production model for news (eMarketer, 2008). Bloggers, for their part and notwithstanding their mission to individualize the news, 'heavily rely on traditional media', according to Richard Davis:

> One survey of blog content found that 69 per cent of blog posts included as a source a traditional media outlet such as the *New York Times*, the Associated Press, or the *Washington Post*. Bloggers rely on traditional media more than they do each other: [the] study found that 64 per cent of the posts had sources coming from other bloggers. (Davis, 2008: 4)

Furthermore, bloggers and journalists are sometimes one and the same person; the two groups overlap significantly (and I will have more on this in Chapter 5) as journalists will use blogs as a forum for presenting the views they are unable to incorporate into a more traditional journalistic format. Davis situates both as members of the 'journalistic community as a whole' and argues that 'as long as journalists see bloggers as potential news sources, and bloggers rely on the traditional media for news, their work will be intertwined, not distinct' (ibid: 36). Indeed, Hindman's research (2007; 2009) suggests that political bloggers probably constitute an elite formation of professional journalists in the USA, and in Australia and the UK there is certainly a significant pattern for high-profile bloggers to have established themselves initially as electronic journalists or newspaper columnists. Even a self-confessed tabloid, sensationalist, blogger, such as the UK's Guido Fawkes, describes himself as 'a campaigning journalist who publishes via a website' (Guido Fawkes, 2008).

Nonetheless, or indeed perhaps because of this close relation, some journalists are critical of what they regard as a lack of accountability in blogs and in citizen journalism enterprises: they point to the variability of editorial control in these formats, and the need to maintain some kind of filter between the citizen journalist or blogger and the final news product (Thurman, 2008: 144–5). As a sign of the danger of dispensing with the editor, 'fake' citizen journalism stories have become a staple component of the mainstream media's news diet. Even such a Web 2.0-friendly location as *Wired* can't resist picking these up. In a story headlined '"Citizen Journalist" Could Face Prison for Fake Jobs Story', they reported that a 'citizen journalist', who posted an erroneous story that said Apple CEO Steve Jobs had suffered a heart attack, is likely to be investigated for attempting to influence the Apple share price:

> ... the erroneous story, which appeared in CNN's iReport – a citizen journalism site pitched as 'unedited' and 'unfiltered' – prompted a sell-off of Apple shares, which dropped to $95.41 from $105.27 between 9:40 am and 9:52 am EST, before Apple denied the report and the stock recovered. (Schiffman, 2008)

Journalists have also registered their discomfort with the personal and self-promoting aspect of these alternative forms of journalism – that is, their readiness to foreground the writer and their opinions – as well as their implicit undermining of some of the fundamental practices of newswriting: breaking the mould of the 'inverted pyramid' model, for one, but also, and more significantly, implicitly breaking with the principles of impartiality, objectivity and the verifiability of information.

Neil Thurman is among those who have consulted the traditional news media for their views on the part to be played by the various forms of user-generated content (the UK Ofcom study [2007] does a little of this too). Among the critical factors that Thurman's interviewees – all senior news editors – mention is simply the volume of material that the user-generated facility in their online presence can produce and, consequently, the heavy demand on the organizations' resources to administer let alone actively moderate them. (Thurman cites the example of the BBC having to deal with 35,000 emails on the day that iconic radio presenter John Peel died [147].) While user-generated content is effectively cost-free for the user, user-generated content initiatives can be expensive for the host organization to run and there is not yet a business model that enables these costs to be recovered from users. The upside is that a number of Thurman's respondents reported that their web-sites have proven 'a useful new source of exclusive content' (149), both in terms of news stories and as components in news coverage – the latter effectively a new form of *vox pop*. In concluding, his survey reflects a grudging acceptance of this new capacity among senior editorial staff in the mainstream media, despite their lingering reservations:

> Journalists and editors had some concerns about user contributions. They felt that there was a need to edit material in order to avoid duplication, keep the standards of spelling and grammar high, select material that was newsworthy with broad appeal and ensure balance and decency. There was also some questioning of the claimed novelty of blogs – a popular mechanism for eliciting reader contributions – and a resistance to their personal tone. Nevertheless, there was no fundamental prejudice against the form, and several publications intended to expand their provision in this area as time and ability allowed. (Thurman, 2008: 154)

An American study has come up with an alternative snapshot as to how this formation of the demotic turn might be integrated into journalists' everyday practice – this, rather than simply displacing traditional formats. A recent research report on the performance of 'the Millennial Generation' (that is, the 18–29-year-old) journalist in the USA revealed a marked generational specificity in their use of new technologies (McClure, 2008). The research found that 100 per cent of the Millennials believe that new media tools are enhancing their journalism (as against 40 per cent of the 50–64 year olds); 87 per cent of the Millennials also believe that bloggers have become important opinion shapers (as against 60 per cent of the 50–64 year olds); 87 per cent maintain that their use of new media enhances their relationship with their audience (as against 42 per cent of the older generation); and 48 per cent used social networking sites such as Facebook to assist in their reporting and to engage with their audiences. What these admittedly preliminary results suggest, according to the report's authors, is that this younger generation of journalists understands how to use the new digital technologies 'effectively in their work, and are pushing the journalism profession as a whole to create a more collaborative, reciprocal, interactive and fluid form of journalism' (ibid.).

While still falling well short of the revolutionary rhetoric of the net boosters, what I have called elsewhere the 'digital orthodoxy' (Turner, 2009b), the professional adaptation of the Millennials nonetheless indicates how journalism practices might mutate over time in ways that will help the profession reconnect with their community and rebuild its faith in the social function of the journalist. The generation gap the research reveals reminds us also that blogs, user-generated content and the like, are evolving practices with a long way yet to run before their role and significance can be confidently understood. The hyperbolic claims made by their advocates have not done these new developments any favours; the predictions used to boost their importance were always likely to overstate what could eventually be achieved. While there is certainly strong evidence that the mediascape has expanded in the volume of material relating to the news, current affairs, and politics generally, and while it is true that some of the traditional sources of news are losing audiences to online ventures that are providing different and alternative points of view, it is also true that many of the reports of this situation exaggerate its actual influence. In particular, and as a major reason for caution in predicting the future of large-scale changes around the globe, academic treatments of the blogosphere and of the shift to online news tend, overwhelmingly, to draw their evidence from specific First World sites – particularly the USA – and thus overlook how uneven is the global distribution of the capacity to make use of these technologies at all, let alone for these purposes. At this stage we need to remember that most of the world's populations do not have access to the online environment.

Entertainment and opinion

I want to move now to another dimension of the shifts in the consumption and production of journalism, and this is to do with a further major shift in the orientation of journalism formats that affects all media. Among the routine news stories published about the consumption of news in the western world is one which points to the paradoxical fact that while young people appear to consume almost no news or current affairs from any medium or platform, they constitute a large and enthusiastic audience for television comedy and satire programmes which focus upon the news, and which depend upon a knowledge of the news for their comedy to be understood. The UK has a number of these (some of which have been sold as formats to other countries – in Australia, *Have I Got News For You* is *Good News Week*, for instance), and Australia has home-grown examples as well, such as *The Chaser*. There is a small sub-genre of sitcoms – *The Hollowmen* (Australia) and *The Thick of It* (the UK) for instance – which depend for their comedy on a sophisticated knowledge of the production of 'spin' as a tactic of policy development and government. The Canadian satiric series, *This Hour Has 22 Minutes* and *The Rick Mercer Report*, have attracted youth demographics to political satire; and Canadian television has long played to a receptive market by targeting the United States as the butt of its political satire, as exemplified by Rick Mercer's (2001) hit *Talking to Americans*. The US itself is currently going through something of a golden era of television political satire, with *The Daily Show*, the *Colbert Report* and a resurgent *Saturday Night Live* having played a high-profile role in the 2008 US presidential campaign (Hamm, 2008). Excerpts from all of these programmes tend to feature heavily in the top-rated clips on YouTube, downloaded in large numbers around the globe. *The Daily Show*, for instance, capitalizes on the USA's hegemony over western popular culture – its continuing function as the transnational popular culture – by attracting a massive international audience online, notwithstanding the fact that so much of what it satirizes is grounded within that country's current national politics. The puzzling and paradoxical implication of this trend is that news may have found a place in an audience's entertainment playlist at the same time as it has lost its place among that same audience's sources of information.

Most of the media reports simply present this apparent paradox for our bemusement: that is, they tell us that the section of the audience with the least interest in traditional current affairs constitutes the primary demographic for satiric programmes focused on news and current affairs. However the Project for Excellence in Journalism has investigated *The Daily Show* to see just how it compares to traditional news and current affairs formats and agendas. They found that it does indeed draw heavily on national political news, but in a highly selective way that 'closely resembles the news agenda of a number of cable news programs as well as talk radio'. Although the show does make 'heavy use of news footage', the purpose, the research agreed, was 'satirical rather than reportorial' (Journalism.org, 2008). That would seem unsurprising, if it were not for the fact that when Americans were asked to name the journalist they most admired in 2007, Jon Stewart – the host of *The Daily Show* – came fourth (Journalism.org, 2008)!

What this seems to reflect is the fact that even though such programmes make use of news or current affairs as a platform upon which to mount an entertainment programme, to their viewers they seem somehow to be participating in journalism. My suspicion is that this occurs because (although they may contain little in the way of new information about current events) the programmes' satiric sketches and other format features express, in one way or another, an opinion on current events. (Or, as Tom Rosenstiel, the director of the PEJ research project puts it, the show is actually making some very serious political commentary, but they 'use humour to do it' [Bauder, 2008].) That opinion, as we witnessed in the effect of Tina Fey's wickedly accurate impersonation of Sarah Palin on *Saturday Night Live* in 2008, does have the capacity to actively contribute to the formal operation of politics. The power and attraction of the programme are reinforced and magnified every time that capacity is demonstrated.

If we think back to Hallin's (1994) general case against contemporary journalism, it may be that there is a very specific formation in relation to this youth demographic. As they have lost faith in the ideals invested in the figure of the objective journalist and in the principled disinterestedness of the news media as an industry, it seems that this sector of the audience is looking for signs of an explicit distancing from, or even a debunking of, such positions rather than their renewal or renovation. The exploitation of an entertainment format, with all the implications of disrespect and irreverence that this carries, as well as the refusal to comply with spurious protocols of objectivity when dealing with an issue of public concern upon which they feel moved to express an opinion, does seem extremely well calculated as a means of speaking to that demographic. It is a strategy that we can also see implicated in the commercial success of Michael Moore (Turner, 2005: 88–92). Far from the move towards these entertainment formats, then, indicating a lack of engagement with public issues, perhaps in a complicated way it indicates a different kind of serious engagement with those issues; for this audience, they are *too* important, perhaps, to leave to a discredited model of journalism.

While there may well be a complex negotiation going on in this sector of the audience in relation to these programmes and genres, however, there is not much evidence of it elsewhere. The trends are clear and uncomplicated. Indeed, it probably goes without saying that news and current affairs formats right across the media have become increasingly indistinguishable from entertainment formats. The bulk (and I mean the bulk!) of our weekend newspapers is now taken up with lifestyle sections, entertainment sections, business and finance sections, lift-out colour magazines devoted (again) to a mixture of lifestyle, celebrity and fashion journalism – with hard news or features restricted to a slim minority of the pages. In most places where it survives, short-form current affairs television has not engaged in serious investigative journalism for years and seeks its audiences through the standard tabloid agenda of celebrity, medical freakery, quack diets or cures for back pain, bad neighbours and opportunistic moral panics (Turner, 2005). Mass-market magazines have been dominated by celebrity for more than a decade, and while talk radio (as we shall see) may derive much of its discursive framework and apparent authority from its increasingly attenuated links with journalism, very few of its actual practices come from there. In general, then, and for a variety of reasons – such as the global restructuring of the media industries in response to increased competition and new technologies – many formats that were once dedicated to journalism have been transformed into entertainment formats. At the same time, as noted above, there is also some movement in the reverse direction as certain entertainment formats have taken on elements of news and current affairs journalism and thereby found a significant youth audience for their hybridized combination.

A key factor here, in my view, is the prominent role of opinion both in these new formats and in the transformations of the old formats. This, too, can be related to major shifts in the commercial organization of the media. In a context within which media outlets and platforms are multiplying and audiences are fragmenting, for many elements of the media the search for a mass audience is fast losing its rationality as the basis for doing business. Even the industry standard of the ratings system for the electronic media is losing its relevance in a fragmenting market. Advertisers have focused on demographics rather than total numbers for a considerable time now, but the public accounting for media performance in television, radio, and even the internet, is still customarily expressed in terms of total numbers – 'bums on seats', or to use the more irritating television industry term, 'eyeballs'. Internally, however, the media industries are increasingly concerned with finding new ways to assess the value of their products for the audiences, their network or provider, and advertisers.

How this plays out for the situation I am describing is interesting. The current market for media audiences in most places and across most media rewards those who can attract and hold a core, committed, constituency; it may be small but it needs to be loyal (and, of course, attractive to advertisers). The basic necessity of entertaining one's core audience – as against attracting a mass audience – has provided a commercial justification for journalism's shift away from the objective, from the consensual, or from addressing one's audience in a way that recognizes its diversity. As we shall see in the next chapter when we move on to talk radio, changes in regulatory structures, particularly in the USA and Australia – but also there seems to be some loosening of their application in the UK – have freed talk radio hosts to ramp up the level of aggression with which they address their callers and interviewees. As a result, the kind of entertainment they offer has become more provocative, more divisive and less interested in any concessions to civility.

The result, in formats such as short-form television current affairs and talk radio as it has developed in the United States and Australia, is that the presentation of information has merged with the presentation of opinion. With the commercial situation as described in the previous paragraph, there is little market incentive to police the boundaries between them by restoring some kind of editorial function or by conforming to the journalistic principles of objectivity or fairness. As the news media face a decline in their credibility as an independent source of authoritative information, and as they compete with other sources of entertainment, the airing of opinion has become a key commercial strategy. This strategy relinquishes the claim to a previous version of authority, that of the impartial professional journalist, and replaces it with the celebrity of the opinionated host, whose attraction as an entertainment is directly measurable through the aggregated choices of the audience. The US TV network FOX is among the pioneers of this strategy; in the presentation of their news channel, they jettisoned the high moral ground of objectivity in favour of promoting the spectacle generated by the presentation of opinionated news. Originally seen as slightly risky because of its disregard for the ethical standards underpinning the professional practice of television news journalism, this has proven a canny commercial move as it has eventually become the top-rated cable news network in the USA. As the mass media markets fragment into smaller slices and demographic niches in response to the expansion in the choice of providers and platforms of delivery, the polarization of community opinions turns out to be a viable means of building both a programme's distinctive identity and a strong core audience.

The political blog, as I noted at the beginning of this chapter, is also a key example of this shift – despite the fact that it is so often cited as an indicator of the political potential of the internet to multiply the points of view and sources of information available to the consumer. Successful political bloggers offer the same entertainment-driven mix of opinion, comment and audience participation as FOX news or talk radio. Indeed one of my colleagues, Jason Wilson, has drawn my attention to the long list of family resemblances between the formats and performance of political bloggers and talk radio hosts. Like their counterparts on radio, these bloggers will usually use the news as a trigger for the presentation of their opinion on a related point; they might hyperlink, or sometimes include a video grab, but the point is not to provide background or information about the issue – rather, it is to use the information as a jumping-off point for the presentation of their opinions. There seem to be some differences between how this is done in various locations (although the blogosphere is so vast, I would admit this assessment is inevitably impressionistic): the UK blogs tend to be less voluble, with a preference for shorter, more satiric or ironic commentary, while the US blogs are more inclined to the long-form rant. Many blogs are also populist in their politics, in the way I want to propose is typical of talk radio in the following chapter, by privileging the common sense of their 'community' of users over the interests of 'elites'. There may be national differences here as well – while conservative blogs dominate in the UK (according to one account, 15 of the top 20 blogs in 2008 were on the right, and only three on the left [Whenman, 2008]), the reverse seems to be true in the United States, with liberal blogs such as Daily Kos among the most popular. On the other hand, Lovink argues that the blogosphere, internationally, skews towards the conservative side: 'the identity circus called the "blogosphere"', he says, 'is not exactly the place where progressive types set the tone' (2008: 1). There also seems to be a widespread view that political blogs have a greater effect on mainstream party politics in the USA than elsewhere, although I am not aware of any research which demonstrates that conclusively.[5]

The tone and conduct of the blogs in each country seem to vary as well. By and large, the US blogs are more deliberately offensive in the way I have outlined above – confirming their 'family resemblance' with the mode of debate employed on US talk radio. Like that of the talk radio hosts, this approach has proven successful in generating comments from readers (which is where most of the more offensive comments are located) and thus in generating news and controversy, which in turn attracts more visitors to a site. A typical recent example of the kind of comment which seems routine on the conservative blogs in the USA is a contribution to the prominent US blog hosted by Michelle Malkin, for instance, which responded to Malkin's criticism of the wife of the Illinois governor, implicated in a scandal involving Barack Obama's Senate seat, (ironically) for her 'unladylike mouth'. The posted comment that the governor's wife was as 'classy and honest as a crack whore', set off a thread of elaborations that ran for several days (Malkin, 2008).[6]

Malkin is also an example of the pattern for many political bloggers from both ends of the political spectrum to develop a celebrity persona, a personal political brand that is both controversial and commercially viable. In Australia, two key right-wing bloggers, Tim Blair and Andrew Bolt, have used their blogs to build a national following that would otherwise be denied them if they depended purely on their metropolitan newspaper columns. Their role as journalists provides a form of news-oriented credibility; their provocativeness as bloggers, however, moves them beyond the territory of the news journalist in order to gain an audience. The format then does constitute a model example of the trends I have been describing here as representing a redefinition of journalism: the merging of news, entertainment and opinion within a format that also invites, enables and responds to audience participation.[7]

Indeed, one of the key ways in which this strategy is legitimated is through the media host's successful interaction with their audience – the continual licensing of the demotic voice as a means of turning opinion into common sense, and of reiterating a programme's identification with that source of common sense. The string of comments one can read in the political blogs is far more extensive than anything which can be made available on talk radio: they provide a continually accessible visual record of the presence of the audience, and require no explicit mediation at all as the contributors are happy to carry on arguing among themselves. Their presence is easily taken for a virtual commons or an open forum, and that can effectively camouflage the fact that all of this is driven by the personal opinions of an individual blogger.

I want to move off the political blog now, although the blogosphere will occupy us for a significant part of Chapter 5. Before moving on, though, I want to suggest that, as journalism attempts to redefine itself, it is in danger of disappearing – leaving behind only a format, a generic frame, for the presentation of entertainment. Possibly the key location for examining this danger, which demonstrates what the consequences can be when traditional journalism survives only as a format of representation, legitimated by the incorporation of the audience into the production of news and current affairs content, is in talk radio. It is now time to devote more detailed attention to this and, consequently, talk radio is the focus of the following chapter where I continue this examination of the current forms of journalism and their relation to the demotic voice.

Notes

1 A typical example of this kind of account is the report jointly produced for the journalism profession by the Media Arts and Entertainment Alliance (the union which represents journalists in Australia), and the Walkley Foundation (an institution set up to acknowledge and support quality journalism), *Life in the Clickstream: The Future of Journalism* (Este et al., 2008).

2 To name a few examples to indicate what I have in mind, though, there is Franklin's *Newszak* (1997), Bromley's *No News is Bad News* (2001), Hermann and McChesney's *Global Media* (2001) (to mention just one from the McChesney catalogue!) and my own account of television news and current affairs in Australia, *Ending the Affair* (2005).

3 Thirty-seven per cent of the Pew (2008) respondents said they used online news services at least three times a week.

4 The contributions of the blogger Salam Pax during the Iraq invasion, who provided an extraordinary source of on-the-ground news to the West, have been widely discussed in the media and in the academy but he still stands out as a highly exceptional example of the citizen journalist/blogger feeding directly into the mainstream media during a major incident or crisis.

5 There is, however, strong evidence of a relationship. *Advertising Age*, in its coverage of the media's treatment of the November 2008 presidential election, noted that the key political blogs The Huffington Post, Politico and Real Clear Politics, grew their audience by 474 per cent, 344 per cent and 489 per cent respectively against September from the previous year (Learmonth, 2008).

6 One can deduce how typical this is of the material on Malkin's blog from the fact that Geraldo Rivera, himself one of the pioneers of so-called trash TV, once reportedly described Malkin as the 'most vile, hateful commentator I have ever met in my life' (Shanahan, 2007).

7 It should be acknowledged that the format of the political blog can vary significantly. There are political blogs built solely around the posts from their host commentator or pundit (Iain Dale's Diary in the UK, for instance, or Andrew Bolt in Australia), there are others which work very much like a newspaper (Crikey.com in Australia, for instance, or the USA's Huffington Post which actually calls itself an internet newspaper and the design of the site reflects that), there are the tabloid-styled provocateurs (Guido Fawkes or Matt Drudge), and many variations in between.

4

Talk Radio, Populism and the Demotic Voice

The politics of talk radio

One of the key issues underpinning the previous chapter – that is, the incorporation of the voice of the public into the production of journalism – is also central to this chapter. Talk radio, at least in the formations upon which I want to concentrate, probably represents the demotic voice at its most aggressive; certainly it is within the media format of talk radio that this voice is most thoroughly embedded. Talk radio has also played a leading role in the merging of news and entertainment that we discussed in Chapter 3. Over time, and in a number of countries, it has been a key factor in the displacement of the journalistic formats of current affairs from radio, as well as exercising a significant influence on the kinds of experiments that have been undertaken with audience participation strategies in television talk shows. Consequently, even while the analysis of radio is itself not often at the forefront of debates in cultural and media studies these days, talk radio does demand concentrated attention in its own right, rather than merely serving as another element to be included within the larger discussion of journalism and the demotic turn. This is reflected, then, in the focus of this chapter. In the first half of the chapter, my research into Australian 'talkback radio' will be used as a grounded example of talk radio's contribution to the public sphere that will, I hope, resonate with other national and industry contexts. The second half of the chapter moves on to a short examination of the leading practitioner of talk radio in the United States in order to introduce a necessary discussion of the relationship between the demotic turn and populism.

Before this, however, it is important to acknowledge that these will constitute quite specific choices from among the range of possibilities that fall under the descriptor of talk radio. Framing my discussion in this way necessarily sets aside those examples which might demonstrate talk radio's more democratic and progressive capacities. That is not to say that I want to argue that talk radio does not have the capacity to function in ways which would be consistent with a process of democratization; rather, my argument is that this is not necessarily inherent in the format nor an automatic outcome of its performance. With this in mind, however, there are certainly examples of talk radio that explicitly pursue democratic objectives. A number of talk radio hosts in Hong Kong, for instance, during the period after the handover in 1997 when the pro-democracy movement was in full swing, played significant roles in advancing public debates about the place of democracy in the future of the Special Administrative Region (SAR) as it was being set up. Francis Lee has made the point that while much western academic analysis of talk radio has focused on its performance within established democracies, it can take on particular importance in 'transitional societies' such as Hong Kong 'where talk radio gained huge prominence in the process of constrained and gradual democratization' (2007: 79). The political and social context in post-handover Hong Kong created quite specific conditions for broadcasters that, he suggests, differed significantly from a situation where the role of free speech is guaranteed. Lee also notes that while talk radio hosts played a crucial role in building support for the pro-democracy movement, this was only achieved by pushing the government's tolerance of their outspokenness to the limit. Indeed, their determination to test that tolerance eventually led to their downfall; during 2004, several of the leading hosts were stood down in response to political pressure – to great public and media outcry (ibid: 92). To discuss this history is to consider far more than the intrinsic political potential of a radio format, and Lee's article emphasizes the point that the attribution of a progressive function to the format must have a conjunctural dimension that can assess this potential within its specific political and historical context.

Given all this, it is interesting to note that even in the case of what he describes as the 'populist' talk show hosts, who were bravely crusading for an opening up of political debate, the performance style remained highly recognizable:

The hosts of the populist shows have a dominant hosting style. They would not refrain from criticizing the citizen callers if they deem the callers' views as unreasonable. They strongly support democratization and they gain popularity largely by their fierce criticisms of the government and other power holders. They tend to see themselves as spokespersons of the common citizens. (ibid: 83)

As we shall see shortly, there are strong continuities in performance style (if not the politics) between these hosts and those we shall later examine in Australia and the United States; this reminds us that a populist politics can work towards a variety of different political objectives in different contexts.

Notwithstanding these similarities in performance, it is also necessary to acknowledge the significant differences between various iterations of the talk radio format. Karen Ross (2004) discusses the format of 'political talk radio' in relation to the UK programme *Election Call*, a 'political phone-in' programme broadcast simultaneously by BBC radio and TV for 12 days prior to the 2001 British general election. This was set up explicitly to provide an alternative to what was regarded as boring, predictable and expert-driven coverage of the national election – and it was aimed at allowing the public to have direct access to politicians without spin-doctors or other intermediaries getting in the way. Ross differentiates this political talk radio experiment from the populist talk radio exemplified by American hosts such as Rush Limbaugh, by noting that the former was intended to provide 'a vehicle for authentic public participation' rather than, as she argues is the case with Rush Limbaugh, simply an 'entertainment commodit[y]' (2004: 788). In an empirical study of the callers who participated in *Election Call*, Ross's research found that her subjects 'definitely *did* subscribe to the view that they were contributing to something meaningful through their participation in the programme' and believed that they were putting forward the views of 'the ordinary voter' (ibid: 788). As we shall also see in a brief account of listeners to regional radio in Australia later in this chapter, Ross's respondents demonstrated that it is possible for this kind of programming to generate the conviction that the ordinary person's voice does count and that a radio programme can indeed play a positive role in assisting citizens in their attempts to hold politicians to account. That said, Ross also admits that her sample of participants was 'not actually representative of the public at large because they demonstrate a desire for

active political engagement that is atypical of most of the electorate'; nonetheless 'they *do* perceive the genre as a genuine public sphere that allows the articulation of alternative (ie *real*
people's) voices' (ibid: 787, emphasis in original).

Political talk radio in the UK, of the kind discussed in Ross's
study, addresses a political and educational class that is very different from the mass audience targeted by the examples I want to
examine below. The major example comes from Australia, where
talk radio has taken on such political and social significance that
it has become a focus of public political debate, as well as of
social and regulatory concern. It provides us with a particularly
striking example not only of how far from a democratizing role
this format can drift, but also of how this can occur without the
need to relinquish any of its legitimizing rhetorics of egalitarian
empowerment – and even in an environment that thinks of
itself as subject to a level of regulation appropriate to the pro-
tection of the public interest.

Talk radio and the Cronulla riots[1]

In early December 2005, in a pleasant beachside suburb of south-
ern Sydney, there occurred what can only be called 'race riots'.
The Cronulla riots pitched local, largely Anglo-Australian residents (that is, Australian citizens from a British background),
against Lebanese-Australian youths from the mainly working-
class suburb of Sydney's middle west. According to the most
credible reports, it expressed tensions that had built up over a
long period among Cronulla residents about what they regarded
as the offensive behaviour of these western suburb youths on the
beachfront. These youths were accused of harassing young women, of
aggressively occupying large areas of the beach to play football, and
of provoking fights with the locals. The flashpoint came when two
Cronulla 'lifesavers' (volunteer lifeguards) were hospitalized after an
altercation with a large group of Lebanese-Australian youths; it was
alleged that the lifesavers were the victims of an unprovoked attack.
Police were accused of ignoring calls for assistance from the
Cronulla community because of political sensitivities about being
seen to be victimizing Lebanese-Australians. Inflammatory reports
in the print and electronic media, a vigorous burst of text-messaging

to mobilize participants on both sides of the dispute, and some opportunistic interventions from local politicians, resulted in a large crowd of Anglo-Australians rallying on Cronulla beach on 5 December 2005. Eventually, fuelled by alcohol, they sought out and attacked anyone of Middle Eastern appearance they could find. Only police intervention prevented serious injury to those targeted. Reprisals followed almost immediately, with carloads of Lebanese-Australian youths arriving from the western suburbs to physically attack residents and trash the shopping centre and suburban streets of Cronulla over several days.

This event shocked Australians; few could have witnessed anything like it before. It also shocked the state government as well. Since the 1970s, Australia has actively pursued a range of immigration and cultural policies, mostly with tacit public acceptance and many highly effective, with the objective of assisting the inclusion of non-Anglo migrants into a multicultural community. A formal commission of inquiry was established, chaired by a former assistant police commissioner, Norm Hazzard, to work through the various accounts of what happened at Cronulla and why. When the Hazzard report was tabled in the New South Wales (NSW) state parliament, it included an analysis of the role that the media, specifically 'talkback' programmes on commercial radio, had played in inflaming community concerns and in disseminating the misinformation which had fed community frustrations leading up to the riot.

This section of the report, prepared by University of New South Wales journalism and media studies professor Catharine Lumby,[2] concluded that 'some elements of the media fed public debate about ethnicity, religion and antisocial behaviour in ways which undoubtedly encouraged, if not actively caused, the perception that Anglo-Australians were under attack by Lebanese/Middle Eastern gangs and that the police force was unable to protect them' (Strike Force Neil, 2006: 35). Crucially, Lumby finds, it was this perception which encouraged the view that the community needed to take some action of its own, leading to the rally to 'reclaim the beach' which precipitated the riot on 5 December.

Prominent among those 'elements of the media' was a talkback host on Sydney AM station 2GB, Alan Jones. As we shall see, talkback programmes have largely displaced more traditional forms of current affairs journalism on Australian commercial radio, with their hosts taking on some of the roles but few of the responsibilities of the journalists they have replaced. Jones has been a particularly influential figure in Australia, with close ties to both the federal and the NSW governments at that time, and he had also run successful campaigns against public and political figures in the past.[3] As the top-rating breakfast show host in Sydney, he was credited by the former Australian Prime Minister, John Howard, with determining the outcome of the 1996 federal election; although there is little evidence to support this view, the claim has achieved mythological status and is indicative of the seriousness with which his political influence is regarded.

This influence has had its commercial as well as its political dimension. In what came to be called the 'Cash for Comment' inquiry in the late 1990s, the regulatory agency at the time, the Australian Broadcasting Authority, found that Jones – despite his characteristic invocation of journalistic independence – had broadcast supportive editorial comment on his programme in return for millions of dollars in fees paid out by major corporations such as banks, telcos and airlines (Johnson, 2000; Turner, 2003). This finding, like numerous other defamation cases which have been resolved against him, did not matter to Jones's core audience: indeed, the more he is brought to the attention of the regulator and the law, the more of a people's hero he seems.

It is not surprising, then, that there should be close scrutiny – from political commentators, legal authorities, academics and the police – of Jones's handling of public comment on the events leading up to the Cronulla riots. In examples quoted in the Hazzard report, Jones read on air, apparently approvingly, an email from a listener who suggested commissioning 'bikie gangs' to meet 'these Lebanese thugs' at Cronulla station and 'send them scurrying back to their lairs'. Jones also provided tacit approval to the caller who said that these people needed 'a rifle butt in the face', and laughed indulgently when 'an old digger'[4] suggested 'if you shoot one, the rest will run'. Although there were occasions when Jones advised listeners not to take the law into their own hands, there were also other occasions when the opposite message was sent out. The gratuitous racial vilification of people of Lebanese background included one comment which implied that Lebanese youths were responsible for all the rapes being committed in western Sydney.[5]

Initially, the fact that the Hazzard report had been completed was denied by the NSW police minister – he claimed it was still in the drafting process – presumably to avoid upsetting an influential broadcaster. When this statement was revealed to be untrue, the minister concerned, Carl Scully, was forced to resign for deliberately misleading parliament. It was a spectacularly high price to pay for attempting to protect a commercial broadcaster who had behaved in a way that was highly likely to be found in breach of the broadcasting code – if not also in breach of the recently introduced anti-terrorism laws that criminalized similar behaviour. When the report was eventually made public, those it had criticized vigorously defended themselves and in turn attacked its authors. Listeners then joined in, arguing that the talkback hosts had performed a public service by expressing what so many others had thought but were afraid to say due to 'political correctness'. Another of the radio hosts concerned, Ray Hadley, told his audience that criticism from an academic such as Lumby was something he 'wore like a badge of honour'.

Over the following year the media regulator, by this time the Australian Media and Communications Authority (ACMA), investigated various formal complaints about Alan Jones's broadcasts during the period leading up to the Cronulla riots. Their task was to decide whether he had breached the broadcasting code of practice which is one of the regulatory requirements upon broadcast licensees under current legislation. On 10 April 2007, the ACMA announced that it had found against Alan Jones on two of the complaints. It stated that Jones had broadcast material which was 'likely to encourage violence or brutality and to vilify people of Lebanese or Middle Eastern background on the basis of ethnicity' (ACMA, 2007). Jones, his employers, and many of his listeners, were outraged, personally attacking members of the ACMA and challenging their authority to make such a judgment.[6]

While most media commentators applauded the findings, there was also significant editorial support for Jones. Although its specialist media columnists all saw it as a 'fair cop', the editorial in the national newspaper, *The Australian*, characterized the regulator's action as an infringement of free speech (13 April 2007,

p. 15) – a line which was also taken in the accompanying op-ed piece written by one of Jones's most well-known supporters (ironically, the former head of the previous media regulatory authority) (Flint, 2007).[7] What seemed most surprising was the fact that the then Prime Minister, John Howard, did not choose to support the regulator his own government had established to ensure that the media serve the public good. Rather, he offered his support to Alan Jones. 'Alan Jones', he said, was an 'outstanding Australian', unlikely to ever incite violence; indeed, his great value to the Australian community, Howard said, was that he was able to 'articulate what a lot of people have thought' (Bodey and Karvelas, 2007: 1). The phrase 'dog whistle politics'[8] has been used to describe this kind of statement, and it was a tactic Howard had used in the past: that is, to covertly indicate a degree of personal sympathy with the cultural and racial intolerance still thriving in some sections of the Australian community.

That Howard should choose this course is a dramatic demonstration of the power that this host, and talkback radio in general, have achieved in Australia. I want now to provide some background to the character of what has become the dominant format through which current affairs is presented on Australian radio before considering some of the political consequences of its rise to dominance.

Talkback in Australia

'Talkback' in Australia is a radio format in which the primary content is generated by listeners' responses to an invitation to phone in and talk 'live' with a host and their audience. There is evidence that Australian talkback is both far more extensive as a format across the broadcasting sector there and also far more thoroughly embedded in the political process than its counterparts in comparable countries such as the UK (although not at the level experienced in the USA). Far more than in television, radio is the medium of choice for most politicians wishing to speak directly to the electorate (Crofts and Turner, 2007; Turner, 2009a; Turner et al., 2006; Ward, 2002). Talkback programmes on the AM band lead the ratings surveys in most Australian metropolitan markets at prime time and talkback components are becoming increasingly common in FM popular music formats as well. Talkback has been a feature of the Australian media since 1967 when it was first legalized; its introduction was delayed by concerns about privacy issues as well as the perceived inadequacy of the available technologies to ensure inappropriate comments could be bleeped out before being broadcast. When talkback did arrive, it was initially aimed at a predominantly female market. It also had what was regarded as an egalitarian mission in that it broke with generations of media convention by taking the views of the average person seriously enough to put them to air: its earliest producer, John Brennan, has described the format as 'God's great leveller' (Bodey, 2007: 15). After experiencing mixed success over the 1970s – the initial enthusiasm resulted in a saturation of the market that in turn led to a significant reduction in the number of programmes using this format (Gould, 2007) – talkback eventually became AM's premier format, providing the sector with its best means of competing against the newly introduced FM music stations over the 1980s.

The process of product differentiation that followed led to the development of a breed of what are commonly called 'shock-jocks'; although these are to some extent in the American mould, they lack the more extreme dimensions we might associate with Rush Limbaugh. Largely, the Australian 'shock-jocks' are 'personalities' or entertainers rather than journalists, often drawn from outside the radio industry, and concentrated in the Sydney market,[9] although some are networked to other cities and regions. Their function is to provoke callers by using a mix of controversial views aimed at polarizing their audience, the shamelessly aggressive and rude treatment of those who call in to disagree with them, and a populist line on all political and social issues. These hosts deliberately set out to be 'bad' – to shock, to provoke and to insult – and to use the aural spectacles their confrontations generate as a means of entertaining their audiences.

Brennan likens the shock-jocks' performance to that involved in 'professional wrestling, just really big acting' (Bodey, 2007: 15). At times, however, this acting has been too 'big', and when this has happened the regulatory authority has stepped in to issue warnings. Under earlier regulatory frameworks, individual broadcasters could be fined or taken off the air. In today's comparatively toothless system, the regulator only has the authority to level sanctions against a radio station as the holder of the broadcasting licence, not an individual presenter. That raises the bar against intervention considerably; punishing large and powerful corporations with the suspension of their operating licence, or the insertion of restrictive conditions into that licence, is not likely to happen without provoking considerable litigation. As a result, the power of the most recent formation of the regulatory body, the ACMA, has yet to be properly tested – hence the pivotal nature of the findings against Alan Jones on Cronulla.[10]

The talkback format has many iterations in the Australian market, however, and it needs to be said that most of them do not set out to be the 'bad boys' of the media industry. The vast majority of programmes on the ABC, the publicly-funded equivalent to Britain's BBC, are locally- and community-based talk programmes which very much operate as a virtual backyard fence for the sharing of gossip, opinion and local concerns. The majority of regional (that is, non-metropolitan) programmes on commercial radio are like this, too: relatively low-key formats hosted by journalists, grounded in local issues most of the time, and conscious of the service they are providing to communities who may be quite isolated in terms of their access to media. Many of the markets served by these regional programmes would not have a locally produced television news bulletin, for instance, or a daily newspaper that dealt with issues going on in the area. Radio is the one medium to have maintained some degree of localism in the journalism provided to such communities in Australia. Unfortunately, even this is under significant commercial pressure, necessitating amendments to a new raft of media laws which hope to limit some of the worst effects of metropolitan media concentration by mandating a minimum level of local content provision in such markets. Interviews with regular callers to these programmes[11] revealed a high degree of support for such programmes as a politically empowering, explicitly democratizing and community-building mechanism. There is usually a news and current affairs core to these, but the facilitation of a community conversation – that is, focused, implicitly deliberative and representative, rather than merely demotic – seems to be at the heart of the audience appeal of this version of the talkback format.

Largely, the metropolitan markets choose to spurn the grassroots or neighbourhood focus as well as its democratic and journalistic function. Their distinctive operation of the format includes a number of quite different models. There are 'celebrity hosts' who attract an audience whose primary goal is to make personal contact with them – achieving access to the world of 'media people' and thus leaving 'the ordinary' behind (Couldry, 2003: 143), or pursuing their parasocial relation with a public figure (Turner, 2004: 23–4). Consequently, the celebrity hosts tend to have a large cast of regular callers who themselves constitute part of the broadcast community of the programme. Calls to these shows frequently commence with a caller fulsomely complimenting the host on his (it is always his) programme or his personal attributes; almost 20 per cent of the calls to one celebrity host my research examined were what I ended up labelling 'fan calls'. The agenda of topics surveyed each day by these hosts tends to vary significantly over time because it is driven almost as much by the callers as by the host. Politics is not the most popular category of topic and most of the talk is about the callers' personal lives: one of the leading celebrity hosts, Sydney's John Laws, had a sentimental self-realization theme that is referenced in his signature phrase – 'keeping the dream alive'.

There are other metropolitan talkback hosts who set out to use the format in ways that do, however, acknowledge the pertinence of the ethical assumptions underpinning the profession of journalism. Their sphere of activity is the provision of news and current affairs and not celebrity or opinion. As noted earlier, one of the by-products of the dominance achieved by talkback formats over the last 20 years in Australia is the virtual eradication from commercial radio of what were once conventional news and current affairs programmes. Under an earlier regulatory structure, radio licensees were required to maintain an independent newsroom, and to provide an element of local current affairs coverage as part of their licence conditions. When radio was de-regulated in the late 1980s, these requirements were relaxed as part of a package of measures promulgated in order to assist the licensees in dealing with a crisis of rising costs; some of these were the result of poor government policy and thus constituted a political liability (Miller, 1997: 65–9). As a result of the introduction of a new self-regulatory regime, radio stations were allowed to lower their investment in news and current affairs – reducing their staffing levels, networking their news or sometimes even sharing newsrooms with competitors, or merely subscribing to a 'rip-and-read' service.

The result was that by the mid-1990s, current affairs (that is, the traditional form of current affairs programming involving journalists, an editorial structure and an attempt to relate stories to the news of the day) had more or less disappeared from Australian commercial radio. Since many versions of talkback did seem to deal with politics and the current issues of the day, and as talkback was thought to be more entertaining than conventional current affairs formats, it became the obvious candidate to fill the space vacated by current affairs programming. Indeed, the ratings success of talkback formats – particularly in the metropolitan markets – reinforced the industry trend against conventional current affairs programming and accelerated its progress.

That said, some of today's talkback programmes, such as that hosted by Neil Mitchell, the ratings leader for the morning slot in Melbourne, still manage to effectively perform the functions of current affairs journalism. Mitchell's programme works closely with the news agenda of the day, its producers follow up stories and pursue lines of enquiry in much the same way that journalists in other media might do, and the programme sets out to inform as accurately as possible by canvassing alternative sides of an issue. Mitchell does not encourage regular callers, there are virtually no fan calls, and he explicitly excludes doing what the industry calls 'live reads' of advertising copy. Live reads are highly sought after by advertisers, who see them as especially credible, but Mitchell's view is that doing live advertisements in the middle of a programme he wants people to regard as serious journalism will only 'demean the authority of the voice'.[12] A former print journalist, he accepts that the change of medium does not release him from the ethical and moral responsibilities he accepted in his previous role. Like a number of other hosts working in this iteration of the format, Mitchell says that his audiences use the programme as a kind of 'filter': a trusted means of sorting through the mass of information available to them today in order to establish which bits of information are important.[13] Given that description of audience interest, the talkback host here is taking on a significant social responsibility.

While hosts such as Mitchell contribute to a flow of information that can be described as socially useful, there is another, larger, genre of 'shock-jock' programmes which also deal with news and current affairs topics but whose objectives are quite different. The common element linking such programmes is that they all deal in opinion rather than information and use these opinions as a means of attracting notoriety, headlines and audiences. The opinions themselves tend to be the product of an opportunistic and highly contingent populism, rather than a set of principled political positions. While this may appear to constitute something like a democratization of media content, given the access it provides for ordinary people to express their point of view (the 'God's great leveller' argument), there is a long history of concern about the anti-democratic potential of populist opinion in the media. More than fifty years ago, Richard Hoggart highlighted the 'rise of "opinionation"' (1958: 201) as a substitute for analysis and judgment, singling it out as a worrying populist tendency in the media and public life. This tendency was particularly evident, he argued then, in the embattled tone and the 'well-known cant of "the common man"', employed by newspaper columnists and leader-writers. Hoggart attacked this tactic as 'a grotesque and dangerous flattery' (ibid: 179) of the public – dangerous because it substitutes a rhetorically constituted '"people" for genuine democratic participation' (Moran, 2006: 560). This observation is still apposite today.

The curious thing about shock-jocks is that, despite their disinclination to seek information in the structured and disinterested way a journalist might, they tend to behave as if they do have personal access to privileged information, their delivery marked by the same discursive markers of authority we would normally associate with journalism. The bogus nature of that authority does not seem to lessen the audiences' respect for their opinions. As long as a host enjoys a significant personal following, whether he proves to be well-informed or not, the evidence would suggest he has the power to act almost as if he is a primary definer of, rather than a commentator upon, social or political issues. The responsibility with which this power is used then becomes a significant social, political and regulatory issue. Unlike the situation in the United States, there are some vestiges of regulation remaining in

Australia, but little in practice to protect the public against this kind of host.

The story of talkback radio's rise to dominance in Australia is a mixed one. While in some ways it has empowered its audiences by acknowledging their voices, in other ways it has reduced the quality of their access to the information a functioning democratic society needs. On the one hand, the development of talkback formats in regional radio has created a new platform for the construction of community as well as for reclaiming some of the news and current affairs content lost to competing commercial imperatives. In some metropolitan markets, also, a small number of talkback hosts have maintained an ethical commitment to the provision of accurate and informed current affairs journalism while seeking to converse with their audiences about current events. On the other hand, while metropolitan talkback's creation of the celebrity host and the populist shock-jock has made radio entertaining in new ways, the format's profiting from the demise of traditional news and current affairs programmes has generated a democratic deficit. The large-scale replacement of the kind of information generated by professional journalists with that generated by an Alan Jones does not serve the Australian community well. This, however, is what the market has produced as a result of industrial shifts over the last two decades, within a context that has been fundamentally shaped by the gradual dismantling of a socially responsive and independent regulatory regime in favour of a more commercially responsive self-regulatory regime. The product is a highly volatile, at times even irresponsible, format which becomes a dramatic example of the transformation of current affairs journalism into a format for opinion and entertainment. As we have seen already, this has presented an opportunity to Australia's politicians and they have taken it; this sector is now the primary outlet for the promotion of political policy to the electorate.

If broadcaster Neil Mitchell is correct, the talkback audience will rely on figures they have learned to trust – and these range from the most professionally disinterested to the most demagogic – in order to filter out the important information from the unimportant information. That seems to be a fundamental feature of talk radio wherever it has been developed. The prominence of politics in the content of so much talkback now increases the importance of this process, while at the same time the manner in which so many hosts deal with political debates does not encourage much confidence in accuracy or independence. Significantly, and to make matters worse, there is now a more narrow range of other media resources available to inform the audience. As noted earlier, commercial television current affairs programming in Australia has largely abandoned the serious examination of politics and society as the two leading prime-time programmes race each other downmarket with stories on back pain, cellulite treatment, cosmetic surgery, unemployed youth, bad neighbours, fad diets and hidden camera scams (Turner, 2005). This places additional importance on the quality and legitimacy of the information provided through those sources that remain. Unfortunately, other than the commercial power available through its choices in the marketplace, there is no longer any formal or statutory means by which the community is able to exercise any significant influence over such considerations. The fact that the regulatory authority now has relatively little oversight of, and few opportunities to influence, the content of broadcast programming, in particular, means that it is simply unable to protect the community interest in relation to events such as Cronulla. Regrettably, the power available to talkback hosts has grown in inverse proportion to the power of the regulatory constraints upon its use.

Over the period of talkback's rise, coinciding as it has with an increasingly market-oriented regulatory regime and notwithstanding the growing public participation in the programming itself, the public access to informed and independent analysis of social and political issues in Australia has diminished. I have written elsewhere (Turner, 2005) about the decline in the credibility and authority of Australian journalism as it has become more thoroughly embedded in the commercial entertainment industry. This decline, paradoxically, has not inhibited those involved from calling on journalism as a source of authority for what they do; indeed, in true populist fashion, they tend to represent their version of journalism as more democratic, closer to the people, and thus as a legitimate corrective to the media of the 'cultural elites'. As a result, in prime-time commercial television current affairs and in the programming of the shock-jocks, the forms and practices of journalism have been captured, disarticulated from their ethical, (fourth estate) foundations, and successfully put to work for commercial ends rather than for the public good.

American populism: talk radio in the USA

It can get worse. The ethical, political and taste concerns which have been raised in relation to Australian talkback radio pale into relative insignificance when compared to the performance of talk radio hosts in the United States. Jones is distinctive in the Australian context because he is relatively open about his goal of exploiting his media profile for political effects beyond the boundaries of his programme. Most of his colleagues would eschew that objective in favour either of simply providing entertainment, or of preserving their objectivity and independence – and, through that latter strategy, something akin to the authority of the old-fashioned journalist. Jones certainly attempts to appropriate that authority while, at the same time, employing the tactics of an opportunistic populism that can swing in a number of directions depending on the prevailing political breeze. Although he does have some aspects of the demagogue in his relation to his audience, one attribute he lacks is an explicit, coherent and consistently argued political agenda.

That is not how leading talk show hosts operate in the United States, however, where the explicit exercise of the partisan political power of the radio host seems now to have become part of the job. Once the regulatory constraints on how controversial issues were dealt with on radio (the so-called 'Fairness Doctrine') were removed by the Reagan administration in 1987, it became possible to say pretty much what you liked on that medium without providing the right of reply to alternative points of view, and without running the risk of a regulatory sanction aimed at maintaining ethical or community standards, or even, it seems, much in the way of legal constraints. Free speech assured, then, the long boom in talk radio followed, with the excesses of both hosts and callers successfully exploited as audio spectaculars which attracted large audiences. The open access provided, and the range of views regarded as suitable for broadcasting as a result of this access, is both remarkable and, to my mind as an outsider, alarming.

Let me give just one, relatively mild, example of what this relaxation of regulation has let loose. Having served a prison term of four years over his role in the Watergate break-in, G. Gordon Liddy now has access to the radio airwaves to present his particular brand of conservative politics to Americans. This has resulted in at least one memorable moment. On 15 September 1994, riding a wave of public anger about federal agencies' management of the Waco siege, Liddy told his radio audience: 'If the Bureau of Alcohol, Tobacco and Firearms insists upon a firefight, give them a firefight. Just remember, they're wearing flak jackets and you're better off shooting for the head' (Bottoms, 1995). Despite the furore this created, and his eventual attempt to retreat from these comments in response to public concern, Liddy remained on air and has apparently maintained some influence. While most would regard Liddy as among the media's political fringe, during the 2008 American presidential election campaign, the revelation of his friendship with candidate John McCain set the liberal blogosphere buzzing in a way that paralleled (in content if not in visibility) Republican accusations about Barack Obama's association with a former Weatherman.

While there have been some colourful and influential US talk radio hosts that non-US readers might recognize (Howard Stern, for instance, comes to mind), the current dominant national figure in American talk radio is one that few outside America will have encountered, Rush Limbaugh. The most popular talk radio host in the country, his audience is dominated by the desirable white male 24–55 years demographic, and he has no interest at all in disavowing or downplaying his political influence. Indeed, his web-site flaunts it:

> The Rush Limbaugh Show is the most listened to radio talk show in America, broadcast on over 600 radio stations nationwide. It is hosted by America's Anchorman, Rush Limbaugh, also known as: America's Truth Detector; the Doctor of Democracy; the Most Dangerous Man in America; the All-Knowing, All-Sensing, All-Everything Maha Rushie; defender of motherhood, protector of fatherhood and an all-around good guy.

> There is a 'consensus' among the American people, who have made this the most listened to program, that it is also the most accurate, most right, and most correct. People who disagree with this are Rush Deniers. (Limbaugh, 2008)

Limbaugh's most devoted followers are referred to, proudly, as 'ditto heads': this reputedly came from the programme's callers routinely beginning their comments with 'ditto to what the previous caller said' (referring either to the content, or else to a compliment to Limbaugh about the show – what I labelled earlier, a 'fan call'), something Limbaugh encourages as a means of saving time. The term has come to suggest that whatever Rush thinks, the ditto heads think too – although Limbaugh himself refutes that interpretation. There is a ditto heads fan culture, serviced by merchandise (bearing the legend 'Ditto Heads: Rush is Right!') such as caps, buttons, keychains, T-shirts, and so on.

While most of those who tune in to the Rush Limbaugh programme are not ditto heads, each day 20 million Americans (Nylund, 2004: 138) enjoy Limbaugh's performance. In terms of the Australian comparison, he covers all possible bases: he is both a celebrity host and a shock-jock but his opinions are given the respect normally accorded to independent journalism, despite their partisan, even demagogic, character. As with Alan Jones in Australia, his domination of his own format does not enable anyone who calls in to do much of the talking. As part of our study of Jones, Stephen Crofts and I analysed a large sample of the transcripts and found that the talkback host spoke for 75 per cent of the time he was on air (Crofts and Turner, 2007)! I haven't yet performed a detailed analysis of this kind for Limbaugh's programme, but reading the archived transcripts on his site makes it clear that he would be clocking up a similar (if not an even higher!) proportion of the airtime. The callers' brief contributions work like triggers to activate a long rant from Rush, producing hundreds of words at a time, usually uninterrupted by any other voice. Callers can only get out a sentence or two before Rush takes over to present his view on whatever issue the caller has raised. 'Empowerment', therefore, doesn't seem like the correct word to describe what is offered to the caller by way of the opportunity to talk to Limbaugh on air. A form of validation or inclusion, perhaps, is a more accurate description, as the caller takes the opportunity to express his agreement with Rush's politics and thereby receive access and sometimes approbation in return.

Like that of most of his colleagues in US talk radio[14] and like that of some of the more prominent political bloggers referred to in the previous chapter, Limbaugh's politics come aggressively from the right, marked by a particular brand of American populism that distrusts all 'liberals', 'elites' and experts, and continually seeks to curb the power of government in order to allow citizens greater control over their own lives.[15] Critics have observed that the leading American talk radio hosts represent 'populism in its purest form, because [they] use direct feedback, calls from listeners, to shape political sentiments' (Mattussek, 1995: 26). Hallin has drawn attention to the importance of populism in the American media, and its deep roots in American popular culture: 'at least since the age of Andrew Jackson, politicians, the press and popular culture have paid obeisance to the wisdom of the People, often contrasting it with the corruption and selfishness of those who hold power' (1994: 91). Writing about television but nevertheless making a point that is just as pertinent to Limbaugh's political function, Hallin goes on:

> The political consequences of [media] populism are complex, and often, in fact, anti-democratic ... [At] times, it causes the media to avoid controversies that seem likely to offend the mass audience, or to jump on the bandwagon of what seems a safe and appealing majority sentiment. Sometimes it manifests itself in 'anti-establishment' themes; television loves nothing more than a story about a 'little guy' who stands up to the 'powers that be'. Sometimes it serves as a resource to the power broker who knows how to play the populist hero. The success of Ronald Reagan in shaping the tone of television ironically owed much to television's populism, because Reagan played the populist hero particularly well, and because television was both fearful of crossing his popular appeal to restore American greatness and irresistibly tempted to adopt that appeal as its own. (ibid: 91–2)

The assumed connection between a form of popular participation and a democratic politics, against which I have been arguing throughout this book, is explicitly inverted here. Indeed, one of the early accounts of the format is entitled 'Tuning in to hate' (Mattussek, 1995), highlighting the fact that utterances aimed at denigrating, intimidating, and inciting hatred and even violence against groups of people on the basis of their sexuality, 'race', ethnicity, gender, political views, and so on, had become routine components of populist discourse within talk radio in the United States (Noriega, 2009). Attempts to exclude this kind of utterance, given the lack of an appropriate regulatory regime to perform such a task, only seem to play into the hands of the programmes' anti-government agenda; they readily dismiss such criticism as motivated by an elite, liberal, 'political correctness'.

It is important to differentiate between the populism of Rush Limbaugh and the like and what I am calling the demotic. Populism is a political discourse, with a specified agenda that legitimates itself through its claim to be the voice of the people. The demotic, too, is 'of the people', but it differs from populism in that it does not necessarily involve an explicit political or social agenda and will have much more than one voice. The demotic is unruly, contingent and potentially cacophonous. As I argued in Chapter 1, while it does seem to me that specific iterations of the kinds of phenomena this book deals with often do turn out to have a politics behind them, it seems to be constitutive of the demotic turn that the precise direction of its politics cannot always be determined in advance. The demotic is, in a sense, discursively empty in the first instance – or, perhaps, more correctly, it is discursively replete in that it includes, theoretically, the full range of possible discourses. The demotic acquires its politics, and the discourses in which they are embedded, in the highly contingent and often opportunistic manner I described in relation to reality TV in Chapter 2. In contrast, while the populism we might identify in Rush Limbaugh's programme is, in its own way, also an opportunistic appropriation of the demotic voice, it makes strategic use of the constructed authenticity of that voice in order to articulate what is in fact an already established political and social agenda.

Limbaugh's performance on talk radio provides an excellent example of how, on the one hand, the demotic turn can prove something of a boon to a populist host, who wants to employ its capacities and its popular credibility as a means of authorizing his public presence. It is ironic, then, on the other hand, that what is actually the empowerment of the host can be made to appear to be something so thoroughly different – namely, to constitute the empowerment of his popular audience as they gain access to the 'media centre' and to the briefest of para-social engagements with their favourite celebrity.

Populism and cultural studies

Cultural studies has its own history of populism, of course. In 1992, Jim McGuigan's book, *Cultural Populism*, diagnosed a condition in cultural studies which, he argued, had the effect of privileging particular media practices and sites of analysis where an argument for a form of progressivism could be mounted – this, at the expense of dealing with the more conservative, regressive forms where, presumably, such an argument was less defensible but where critical analysis was probably more politically necessary. We looked for progressive readings of commercial television game shows, say, rather than criticize the regressive class politics underpinning the audience address of the UK's *Sun* newspaper. Such a habit of analysis and examination tended to privilege those aspects of popular culture that could be read as transgressive or, as McGuigan put it, which supported a 'consumptionist' view of popular culture that was excessively optimistic about the audience's productive relation to the text.[16] McGuigan's admittedly polemical book was intervening in debates about the usefulness of interpretation and textual analysis, implicitly posed against the benefits of political economy, so it reflected the debates of the time in highly nuanced ways. Mostly, we could be forgiven for thinking of these as debates which have been resolved and left behind us. McGuigan's goal of promulgating a 'critical populism', which can 'account for *both* ordinary people's everyday culture *and* its material construction by powerful forces beyond the immediate comprehension and control of ordinary people' (1992: 5, emphasis in original), does seem to describe the dominant practice in cultural and media studies today.

However, some contributions to the debates over the cultural function of reality TV, for instance, in recent years reflect a similar positioning to that which McGuigan criticized in 1992. Understandable, to be sure, because of the need to problematize the issues underlying the many large-scale media panics about reality TV which have been generated from opposing points of view, but nonetheless also vulnerable to the kind of charge made in McGuigan's book more than a decade ago. I see elements of this kind of positioning more generally implicated in what has become almost a reflex, and I think certainly largely unexamined, attribution of a democratic politics to the shifts in popular culture I am describing in this book as the demotic turn. As a result, the examples we have looked at in this chapter seem to me to be cases where cultural and media studies should be taking a far more critical approach – that is to do with exposing the abuse of the media's power, rather than focusing on the personal benefits provided to the consumer in order to win their assent to the larger structural conditions. So, while there is certainly a sense of dynamism in these talk radio formats, for instance, which would encourage their being seen as a lively expression of popular culture, that is not enough, in my view, to defend them against a careful examination of what might in some instances be described as their poisonous cultural and political functions. Where the demotic voice is so overwhelmingly enlisted in support of a political populism that is intolerant, anti-democratic and demagogic, it is hard to argue that the medium which enables this to happen is serving us well. When the programming concerned has also gained its prominence and popularity through the displacement of a more responsible format for informing the public, there is even more reason for cultural and media studies to put the political and cultural deficit under scrutiny.

In my view, the condition that McGuigan diagnosed in 1992 was well on the way to a cure by the time his book was published, and I would not necessarily agree with all aspects of his diagnosis as outlined in it. However, it did reinforce criticisms of what had been in danger of becoming the default setting for cultural studies' examination of the media and that was producing an increasingly complacent account of the media's political effects. Such an account was easily mobilized because of cultural studies' foundational concerns with resisting elite and conservative accounts of the media that had their own default settings. However, an unforeseen effect of the insistence on understanding the media's function in its own terms, or in a sympathetic relation to the uses made of it by its audience, was the ensuing implication that the media's influence was largely benign because its meanings could be easily resisted or 'made over' by the active audience. To put it crudely in the terms in use at the time, capitalist ideologies could be resisted through the audience's negotiated or resistant readings of the popular texts in which these ideologies were embedded. While this certainly aligned with cultural studies' implicit respect for the popular and its related scepticism about the assumption that popular audiences were 'cultural dopes' – both of these positions that made the cultural studies enterprise possible in the first place – it ran against the grain of another key plank in the cultural studies' platform: its function as a critically and politically engaged mode of analysis.

I would argue here that we are now encountering an analogous situation in the manner with which cultural and media studies have dealt with the political possibilities of new media – and in particular with the potential of user-generated content online. The focus upon consumption, agency and interactivity seems to skew the debate once again in ways that distract attention from the larger structures which contain these practices and relations, and thus privilege highly optimistic and in some ways poorly historicized readings of the implications of the growth of new media, interactivity and user-generated content.

In the following chapter, I want to focus on cultural and media studies' discussion of user-generated content. There are two primary reasons for this. The first is that, notwithstanding the criticism I make of their discussion within the academic literature, they still seem to be the most promising location for the democratization arguments I have identified with Hartley (1999), Jenkins (2006), and so on. The second is that nonetheless these arguments need to be given a more critical interrogation than has so far been the case. It would not be hard to come to the conclusion that, for the current generation of cultural and media studies students and scholars, interactivity and user-generated content online is 'cool' in the way that the sub-cultural style of punk, the consciously constructed public persona of Madonna, or the cult pleasures of TV's *Buffy the Vampire Killer* were 'cool' for a previous generation. That comparison should give us pause and suggest we need to be looking a little more closely at the evidence of, rather than the rhetoric about, the political implications of the rising trajectory of these cultural practices before we too easily take their signs for wonders.

Notes

1 A fuller version of this case study is published as 'Politics, radio and journalism in Australia: the influence of talkback', in *Journalism: Theory, Practice and Criticism* (10(4) August 2009).

2 I am also named as a consultant in this report.

3 One of the more chilling examples cited in Chris Masters' *Jonestown: The Power and Myth of Alan Jones* (2006) is the resignation of the reformist NSW Police Commissioner Peter Ryan who had been put under sustained pressure from Jones's programme.

4 This is a vernacular term used to refer to Australian soldiers, particularly those who fought in the two World Wars.

5 The background to this is complex, but there had been a sustained moral panic about a series of vicious and apparently racially motivated rapes in western Sydney some years earlier. When the perpetrators, Lebanese-Australian youths, were given unusually harsh sentences, community opinion was divided between those who applauded this outcome and those who felt it was a response to racialized community pressure and thus contributed to a demonization of those from Lebanese backgrounds. Jones's comment came in response to a caller who suggested that there could be two sides to the Cronulla issue and it may not simply be the fault of people of Middle Eastern appearance. Jones replied with the (inaccurate) claim that 'we don't have Anglo-Saxon kids over there raping women in western Sydney'.

6 In one statement, Jones noted indignantly that he had been a referee for ACMA's chair, Chris Chapman, in a number of job applications; the selection of this detail seemed to imply that Chapman owed him his loyalty as a result and that his subsequent behaviour was rank ingratitude (Bodey and Karvelas, 2007: 1–2). As Chris Davis, in a letter to the national daily, *The Australian*, put it, Jones apparently thought he had Chapman 'in his pocket' (13 April 2007, p. 15) and was furious when he found out he hadn't.

7 As we will see later, when we move onto the American example, this principle is also invoked there to defend the aggressiveness with which talk radio hosts express their views.

8 The phrase is used to describe a political utterance that 'involves sending a particularly sharp message which calls clearly to those intended, and goes unheard by the rest of the population' (Poynting et al., 2004: 153). In this instance, the hidden message is support for a discriminatory view of Muslim-Australian cultures.

9 While talkback itself is ubiquitous, it does seem as if certain markets are more receptive to the shock-jock format; Sydney has the highest number of them in prime time, but Melbourne has proven resistant to them. Sydney shock-jock Stan Zemanek was tried in a prime daytime slot in Melbourne, but only lasted a year.

10 Recourse to criminal law might actually prove more effective; in the case of one host in Adelaide, his comments to one caller were so offensive they resulted in a successful prosecution that briefly put him behind bars.

11 These were not part of a formal research process, but an opportunity that arose during a series of on-air interviews with talkback hosts.

The hosts responded to questions about callers' motivations by asking their regular callers to phone in and discuss it with me on air; this eventually became an opportunity I requested from them and most of the hosts were happy to cooperate.

12 Personal interview with the author, 10 November 2006.

13 Personal interview with the author, 10 November 2006.

14 'In the top 257 radio stations, owned by five major companies, more than 90 per cent of the talk show hosts were conservative; in terms of the number of hours aired the ratio stood at ten-to-one conservative to progressive'. More than 50 million Americans listen to talk radio each week (Hamm, 2008: 37).

15 Suspicion of the very idea of government seems to be one of the articles of faith in right-wing American populism. One commentator reports that the introduction to the programme hosted by Detroit's Mark Scott, one of Limbaugh's competitors, uses an opening coda spoken by a child which says: 'I love my country but I fear my government' (Kay et al., 1998: 12). Scott himself has an especially extreme line on this peculiarly American preoccupation – 'The American dream', he says, 'will be recaptured when Americans eventually see that you can live without government' (ibid: 19).

16 While he never actually gives us a working definition of this approach, it does seem to be what he means when he refers to an '*uncritical* populist drift in the study of popular culture, a discernible narrowing of vision and fixation on a self-limiting set of issues' (1992: 5, emphasis in original).

5

Revenge of the Nerds: digital optimism and user-generated content online

Cyberenthusiasms

In the last chapter of *Haunted Media* (2000), his fascinating history of 'electronic presence' from the late nineteenth century to the beginnings of television, Jeffrey Sconce turns towards some of the current fashions in contemporary media analysis in order to demonstrate the value of a slightly longer historical perspective than had so far been customary in their treatment. Dealing with the 'cyberenthusiasms' of the late 1990s, as 'cyberspace replace[d] television as postmodernity's technological dominant', his account reminds us of what turned out to be a brief, if nonetheless lively, moment when the discussion of the postmodern implications of computer-generated 'virtual realities' and 'virtual subjectivities' were all the rage:

> In the zeitgeist of cyberculture, promoted by both new-tech gurus in the academy and the editorial board of *Wired*, electronic postmodernity is no longer a lamentable 'condition', but is instead a hip and exciting lifestyle in which those who are willing to shed the illusion of the 'human' will be rewarded in the emancipating splendour of techno-bodies and the enlightened consciousness of 'virtual subjectivity'. (Sconce, 2000: 202)

Emerging from academic and industry arguments to do with the development of virtual realities and virtual personas performed through multi-user computer games, and given popular celebrity by their being embedded in sci-fi fantasies such as the (1999) Hollywood film *The Matrix*, there was quite a fuss about this – even while the proportion of the world's population who would ever experience virtual realities has turned out to be very small indeed.

Today, of course, most of us can barely remember this moment, and would find it very difficult to answer Sconce's rhetorical question – 'how can we explain contemporary media theory's enthusiastic and often naïve investment in the discorporative fantasies of cyberspace?' (ibid: 206). Sconce himself deals with the question by pointing to the academic debates about subjectivity current at the time, to which, he suggests, the notion of virtual subjectivity presented a particularly attractive 'coda':

> Having dethroned the bourgeois subject and revelled in the decentering of the postmodern subject, contemporary theory latched onto the exciting fantasy of the malleable cybersubject. For an intellectual circle devoted to the idea that subjectivity is ultimately a fragile and variable historical concept, technologies that promise to craft, exchange, transmute, and otherwise conjure subjectivity would of course have immense appeal. Thus were the humanist illusions of traditional metaphysics replaced by the technological illusions of electronic presence. It is almost as if, unsettled by the subject's historical variability, contemporary theory looked to the cybertechnologies as both a validation of its model of the constructed subject and as a means of deliverance from that model's potentially alienating implications. (ibid: 207)

Sconce points out how accepting the power of the new technologies to 'engineer' new subjectivities and realities implicitly dismissed the social and political mechanisms 'originally posited as producing subjectivity in the first place'. Today, we might well share his incredulity at this development: 'are the experiences and categories of gender, race, sexuality and class really so disposable' he enquires, 'that they can be escaped or even significantly disrupted by a few hours in cyberspace' (ibid: 208)? At the time, though, this kind of question would have been regarded as spoiling all the fun.

Sconce concludes by noting how daunting is the problem of understanding the complex, dense, 'increasingly invasive' and 'truly relentless' signifying environment created by electronic media, and how tempting it is therefore to ignore engagement with the detail of the overdetermining social and economic structures in order to 'abstract' the whole thing 'into a religious vision of virtual omnipresence' (ibid: 209). He reminds us, though, that such an ahistorical vision must eventually be superseded:

> We would do well to remember, however, that 150 years from today, it is doubtful anyone will be discussing or even remember our current debates over simulation, hyperreality, cyborgs, cyberspace, techno-bodies, or virtual subjectivity, except perhaps for a few baffled historians interested in the peculiar mystifying power that a certain segment of the intelligentsia invested in their media systems. (ibid.)

The vigorous debates of the late 1990s, he concludes, will become the 'fantastic folktales' of the past and, even from this short temporal distance, it seems they are well on their way on that destination.

Sconce's book is a rewarding and revealing study, and these contemporary comments are really only a postscript to its history of the mythologies surrounding modernity's engagement with electronic media. However, they do provide a very useful reality check against some of the directions being taken in contemporary media studies debates. They help to alert us to the possibility that we are in danger of making similar errors in our dealings with the fashionable narratives about the new media at present – to do with the demise of traditional (or 'legacy', or even more hubristically, 'heritage'[1]) media, the liberalization embedded in the alternatives, and the consequent emancipation of media audiences through blogging, DIY video, user-generated content, and the like. The lack of an historical imagination, ironically, undermines many of the claims of an historic break, rupture or discontinuity between new media and their predecessors, suggesting that some of them, at least, are bound to take their place eventually alongside Sconce's 'cyberenthusiasms' of the 1990s.

There is, nonetheless, plenty worth talking about in the growth of these new media and the opportunities it provides for producers and consumers, as well as for those who think they are both. And there is more at stake here than just avoiding the kind of error mentioned above; these issues are to do with what might well be a radical remaking of the mediascape and in particular a significant reframing of the terms upon which we, as citizens, engage with the media. It is important then that we get this right, and understand the changes that are now under way. Towards that end, in this chapter I want to address some of the more utopian arguments about the emancipatory, liberalizing and democratizing potential of the new media in order to critically assess the evidence that there are new forms of interactivity now in play which offer an increased and meaningful public participation in the changing cultures of media production and consumption.

Digital optimism

It could go without saying that the internet is the prime location for those in cultural and media studies who would argue that the contemporary spread of media choices and the new opportunities of access and interactivity constitute a form of democratization. Indeed, it has become almost a commonplace of public opinion to claim that the internet has given voice to those who were previously voiceless and provided citizens with an unprecedented degree of participation in the media; this dimension of the internet's social and political potential even achieved the status of legal fact when no less an authority than a Supreme Court judge pronounced it to be a 'unique democratizing medium' (Hindman, 2009: 3).

As we have seen in a number of locations throughout this book so far, the development of new kinds of interactivity and participation has not only altered the balance of power between the producer and the consumer in some locations, it has also blurred the distinction between these two functions. Indeed, this shift has been so pronounced that new terms, such as 'produser',[2] have been coined to describe a consumer who creates their own content and distributes it online through video aggregator sites such as YouTube, social networking sites such as Facebook, or via blogs (Bruns, 2008a; Tapscott and Williams, 2006). However, so much attention has been attracted to these shifting relations that there is now something of a glut in projections of a future based upon them. This is the case not only within the academy but also within the media industries themselves. At the 2008 National Association of Television Programming Executives (NATPE) conference, I listened to leading industry professionals who confidently proclaimed the death of traditional media such as television and their replacement by user-generated content online and on mobile devices, at the same time as programmes were being bought and sold to serve a national television market that was to grow by 4 per cent over the next quarter!

Outside of the hothouse of industry debate, and while no-one denies that we are witnessing a potentially significant development, it is also demonstrable that, while the rise of the 'produser/prosumer'[3] has achieved significant publicity because of its novelty and newsworthiness, such activity constitutes an extremely small proportion of the full range of media consumption and production around the globe. In terms of scale, it is not that significant. In relation to participation through blogging, for instance, internet historian and activist, Geert Lovink, invokes the 'so-called 1% rule, which says that if you get a group of 100 people online then one will create content, 10 will interact with it (commenting or offering improvements), and the other 89 will just view it' (2008: xxvii). In relation to those who upload their own video content onto YouTube, the figure is even lower – less than half of 1 per cent of visits involve posting videos (Miller, 2009: 78). Few would argue with these figures and therefore much of the importance of the claims made for the 'produser' lies in the projections made about what kind of role they will play in the future, rather than in the evidence of what they are doing now. Typically, it has to be said, such projections have tended towards the hyperbolic, overstating the current dimensions of the trend while drawing conclusions about the possibilities for the future from a selective geographic sample which reflects the concentration of such activity in the USA. In weighing up the demotic against the democratic, as we have done throughout this book, it is important that we critically examine the available evidence of, rather than merely the prevailing opinions about, the scale and nature of the rise of user-generated content online for its political, cultural and industrial potential.

This is especially important because there is such a strong current of digital optimism around (in the industry, in the academy, among policy makers, and even among the general public) which predicts a dramatic shift in all kinds of potentialities as a result of what is understood as the consumer securing increased control over the production and distribution of media content. What I have called earlier on in this book the 'digital orthodoxy' welcomes this as a significant step towards reining in the excessive power of mainstream, elite, media organizations. The growth of user-generated content, and particularly the rise of the blogger, has fuelled predictions of a grassroots takeover of media space. The persuasiveness of these claims, and their take-up within the academy, has resulted in a widely circulated proposal to reorient the established discipline of media studies (the so-called Media Studies 1.0) around 'Media Studies 2.0' (Gauntlett, 2007). Media Studies 2.0 (the title refers to the user-oriented capacities of Web 2.0) differentiates itself from traditional media studies by foregrounding digital media and the newly interactive audience, and directing attention away from media platforms such as broadcasting in order to focus more closely on the so-called 'long tail' (Anderson, 2006) of narrowcast, niche-marketed, independent and DIY projects. Underpinning the rationale for Media Studies 2.0 is an old media/new media division in which (and I'll admit this is crude, but it is sufficient for my purposes here) the old media is corporate, bullying, exploitative, elitist and anti-democratic, while the new media is grassroots, collaborative, independent, customizable, empowering and democratic. The traditional media studies' focus upon industries and institutions is displaced by a new media focus on the 'produsing' consumer, customized content and the individualized audience where, undeniably, there have been significant and dramatic shifts in both provision and behaviour.

The enthusiasm for this new order is understandable, and its ideals worthy, but in the rush to celebrate Web 2.0's potential some perspective has been lost. The political empowerment promised to consumers is largely based on the expansion of consumer choice, the provision of interactivity and the corresponding rise of the produser. We need to remember that, in practice, these have remained limited developments. In one of the relatively few attempts, so far, to provide empirical evidence for the political effects of an interactive and participatory internet, political scientist Matthew Hindman's recent research on politics and the blogosphere advises caution about optimistic projections of political empowerment. Too often, he cautions, 'normative debates about the Internet have gotten ahead of the evidence' (2009: 18). His findings underline, for instance, the importance of recognizing the difference between who gets to speak on the internet, and who gets to be heard. Rather than the internet amplifying and multiplying the number of voices to be heard, the fact is, he says, that on it, 'the link between the two [that is, who speaks and who gets heard] is weaker than it is in almost any other aspect of political life' (ibid: 17).

As we shall see later on, Hindman is unusual in having generated significant empirical evidence to support his arguments, but he is not alone in expressing scepticism about the projected political significance of the online environment. Lev Manovich, for instance, agrees that academic discussions of the interactive internet have given 'disproportional attention' to 'certain genres such as "youth media", "activist media", "political mash-ups" – which are indeed important but do not represent the more typical usage of hundreds of millions of people'. The skewing of attention in this way carries significant consequences, Manovich argues:

> In celebrating user-generated content and implicitly equating 'user-generated' with 'alternative' and 'progressive', academic discussions often stray away from asking certain basic critical questions. For instance: to what extent is the phenomenon of user-generated content driven by the consumer electronics industry ... To what extent is [it] also driven by social media commentators themselves – who after all are in the business of getting as much traffic to their sites as possible so they can make money by selling advertising based on their usage data. (2008: 35–6)

The need to take on board such questions, as well as to properly examine the institutional and industrial continuities between new and old media, has not been much considered during the production of digital optimism. Indeed, its production has been assisted by an alignment between sectors and interests one would usually expect to adopt quite divergent points of view. Just as the technologies driving the development of a newly accessible media are themselves converging, the opinions of media, business, consumer electronics and web industries, consumers themselves, and media studies academics, have also converged in their celebration of content created and exchanged by users (ibid: 35). As Henry Jenkins notes, 'convergence culture' is both a top-down, corporate-driven process and a bottom-up, consumer-driven process:

> Corporate convergence coexists with grassroots convergence. Media companies are learning how to accelerate the flow of media content across delivery channels to expand revenue opportunities, broaden markets, and reinforce viewer commitments. Consumers are learning how to use these different media technologies to bring the flow of media more fully under their control and to interact with other consumers. The promises of this new media environment raise expectations of a freer flow of ideas and content. Inspired by these ideals, consumers are fighting for the right to participate more fully in their culture. (2006: 18)

While the consumer-driven end of the process is the focus of Jenkins' narrative in this instance, it is also important to recognize the role that powerful commercial interests have played in generating the hyperbole that has popularized the promise of digital media and the new roles these offer to interactive consumers.

As a consequence of this broad-based convergence of opinion, however, many of the discourses popularized by the digital optimists have begun to take on a life of their own. Indeed, digital optimism has begun to exhibit one of the characteristics we noted in Chapter 1 while discussing another widely promulgated media discourse – that of tabloidization. As it is taken up as a popular discourse, digital optimism is becoming almost infinitely expandable in its cultural, social, political and economic ramifications. Symptomatic of this would be the title of Tapscott and Williams' business guide-book about digital technologies, prosumers and the like, *Wikinomics: How Mass Collaboration Changes Everything* (2006). Not 'lots of things', mind — 'everything'. Similarly, Clay Shirky's popular book on digital media's potential for social/corporate (the elision is significant) organization, *Here Comes Everybody: The Power of Organizing without Organizations*[4] (2008); again, those who are 'coming' are not just the well-educated, culturally capitalized, early adopters, but 'everybody'. Such titles illustrate the popular currency of digital optimism; books on business, management and marketing, self-help publications and mainstream cultural commentary all exploit it. The result has been to generate a high level of newsworthiness and thus a particular kind of legitimacy for the ideas they contain.

Helping to drive the public interest in these ideas is their relatively uncritical celebration of the claims made for a new era of consumer choice and consumer sovereignty (Brabazon, 2008). I would have to register some concern at the disingenuousness of this. One of the characteristic discursive tactics of neo-liberal administrations around the world over the last decade or so has been the strategic conflation of consumer choice with the principles of democracy: in all kinds of contexts, the proliferation of choice and access has been accompanied by assurances that the consequences will be more inclusive, democratic and empowering. Mostly, such tactics have been used to justify policies which have shifted the responsibility for the provision of services from government to private industry or the consumer – privatization programmes, 'user-pays', outsourcing, and so on. In the case of the online environment (as with all the others) an opening up of access comes with a financial cost, which means that some sections of the community actually don't have a choice at all.

Why have such considerations not been more routinely noted in the academic, if not the popular, literature, and why does what Hindman calls the 'myth of digital democracy' get such a rails run? So far, there is little more than anecdotal evidence which might tell us how these developments are actually playing out in specific contexts. There is, of course, the daily spin from the industries concerned and one would have to say that this tends to be uncritically recycled in ways that are not typical of the way the academy has treated other media industries in the past. Perhaps those academics and commentators engaged in examining the situation for us believe, sincerely, that their own personal experience is itself a powerful source of the evidence required. To some extent, this is understandable in such a cutting-edge area where change is dynamic and rapid, and where the recent nature of each new development means there is very little in the way of conventionally authoritative academic sources upon which the writer may draw. Perhaps, also, academic commentators have been encouraged by the interest in their views coming from the commercial sector. As early adopters of these technologies (precisely the 'nerds' of my chapter title), they have found themselves in an unusual position for a humanities or social science academic: they are not only sought out by their academic colleagues for their views on the possible social effects of these new media, but they are also recognized by industry entrepreneurs as sources of valuable knowledge about the technologies themselves. What this can do is involve the academics in an informal alliance with industry entrepreneurs and that, in turn, opens up at least two possibilities – that their advice will influence the business plans of these enterprises, hopefully in socially beneficial as well as commercially successful ways, or that their work will become complicit with the commercial or managerial interests of those same enterprises. While I am sure the first possibility would be the motivating one, you would have to predict that the second possibility is the most likely eventual outcome.

There is also the simple fact that the digital optimists appear to have a significant personal and intellectual investment in these new developments and this stands in the way of raising such issues. In more instances than is the case with the academic analysis of television, say, or of the film industry, this investment appears to influence what arguments get made. A significant proportion of the academic engagement with digital optimism is reminiscent, as I noted at the end of the previous chapter, of the kinds of individual preferences (or blind-spots) that were allowed to drive media and cultural studies research in the late 1980s and early 1990s towards those cultural forms which were valued by the researcher concerned according to their own interest in those who used them (Frith, 1991; McGuigan, 1992).

As noted earlier, there is a lack here of an historical dimension, one which would inevitably produce perspective and a sense of proportion, in much of the academic discussion of Web 2.0. There also seems to be a related weakening of the commitment to the appropriate use of evidence in advancing arguments about the digital present and its future. Indeed, this may be developing into a generic characteristic of academic argument in this area: the habit for projections of the digital future to 'look inward to other Web 2.0 hyped-up sources as evidence for their arguments rather than outward to analogue history' (Brabazon, 2008: 18). As Toby Miller has put it, it is as if industry 'hype in and of itself *is* evidence' (2009: 74, emphasis in original). An aspect of this habit is the emerging practice of referencing opinions posted on blogs as if they constituted authoritative evidence.[5] The kind of thing I have in mind is where a researcher makes an assertion which is referenced to a blog, implying that the blog will provide evidence to support that assertion. When you look at the blog, however, all you have is an expression of the blogger's opinion, with little in the way of verifiable or authoritative evidence. I have come across this in publications from researchers whose work I respect and have used with confidence in the past,[6] which raises the possibility that it represents a worrying shift in what is deemed to be acceptable academic research practice.[7] Furthermore, one can't help but note the fact that referring to the blogosphere as a means of supporting academic argument is strikingly consonant with the rise in the authority and currency of opinion that I highlighted in my account of the redefinition of journalism in Chapter 3.

What seems to be happening here, and within the discursive field I have labelled as digital optimism in general, is that some of the lines between media activism, publicity and promotion, and academic analysis have blurred. The new media area, connected as it is to major international academic, intellectual and activist networks aimed at resisting the power of 'Big Media' and championing a more democratic relation between the media and users as well as (interestingly) to an avant-garde directed towards developing new media or multimedia arts and (even more interestingly) to entrepreneurs within the new media industries, seems to have been heavily colonized by this trope. The rights these academic-activists wish to champion and defend are possibly those I would also champion and defend, but the adoption of an activist approach to academic research will not help us, in the long run, to accurately understand the changing cultures of media consumption and production.

Reality check

What is to be done about this? We can start by factoring in some information that should complicate the picture a little. Let's begin by doing a bit of a reality check on claims that user-generated content online is set to soon replace traditional media such as television (Bruns, 2008b). The (2008) Nielsen 'Three Screens' report, which looked at television, online video and mobile phone usage in the United States, provided us with some indicative figures for that market. Released in May of that year, it found that watching TV in the home had increased by 4 per cent since 2007,[8] totalling 127.15 hours per month; this was augmented by a further 5.50 hours watching time-shifted television programming. Use of the internet had increased by 9 per cent over the year, to a total of 26.26 hours per month. While watching video online represented less than 10 per cent of the total usage of the internet, nonetheless 73 per cent of the sample did this for a total of 2.19 hours per month. The picture here, then, is of a steady rise in use of the internet and watching of video online, but in terms of actually challenging the number of hours spent watching the traditional medium of television the comparison is, at the moment, risible. Globally, of course, there is no question that broadcast television remains overwhelmingly the dominant medium for the majority of the world's population (Straubhaar, 2007) and in some countries, India for example, it is undergoing a massive expansion (Athique, 2009).

There is also recent research on the proportion of consumers who generate their own content or participate in online conversations, which supports the rule of thumb I quoted from Geert Lovink earlier on. Rubicon, a US marketing firm, found that, even now, only 1 per cent of consumers are enthusiastic producers of content. They also found that what might look like an open conversation on blogs is therefore dominated by that same 1 per cent of participants. As a result, they point out to their marketing clients, it would be wrong to regard the online community as directly reflecting the opinions or interests of the average 'customer'; rather, they reflect the opinions of the enthusiasts (LaFetra, 2008). This must qualify claims that the blogosphere has provided an accessible, democratic and open space for ordinary citizens.

The really dramatic growth, and therefore where much more work needs to be done to properly investigate the claims being made, seems to be in the numbers who participate in social networking sites. Manovich cites reports that MySpace has moved past 300 million users worldwide, with roughly a third of these from the United States. He also cites Wikipedia figures which claim that 90 per cent of South Koreans in their twenties (that is,

25 per cent of the total population of South Korea) use the South Korean social networking site, Cyworld (2008: 34). The scale of participation is clearly significant, although more so in some countries than others. Even in relation to what is regarded as a global network, variations in online participation around the globe are primarily shaped by domestic, rather than transnational, communications infrastructure and policy environments: South Korea, for instance, has extremely high-speed broadband and almost universal internet access. This is a useful reminder of how contingent these developments are, and therefore how inadequate it is to simply focus upon the determining potential of the technology, rather than upon the social, cultural, political and regulatory context within which it must operate, when making projections into the future.

Among those positions most in need of a reality check has to be the celebration of the online environment as a widely accessible, democratizing, political space. While the growth of political debate through the media, clearly, carries benefits for a democratic polity, the claims made for the internet – and particularly for the blogosphere – have in some cases been quite dramatic and thus demand closer investigation. Matthew Hindman's (2009) research, referred to earlier, undertakes that investigation: it asks whether the internet is democratizing politics, whether the blogosphere has made the public sphere more open and inclusive, and whether open access to the internet has affected media concentration and thus the dominance of mainstream media. Hindman is a political scientist who also understands the technical computing logics which structure our use of the internet. His research is confined to the United States and it does not address social networking sites or the production of entertainment content (I will discuss YouTube and social networking in the next section of this chapter). The group of research projects which inform his (2009) book, *The Myth of Digital Democracy*, use data provided by the international monitoring company Hitwise in order to analyse the content and use of more than three million web pages.[9] What he finds is not at all what the digital optimists would expect:

... [W]hen we consider direct political speech – the ability of ordinary citizens to have their views considered by their peers and political elites – the facts bear little resemblance to the myths that continue to shape both public discussion and scholarly debate. While it is true that citizens face few formal barriers to posting their views online, this is openness in the most trivial sense. From the perspective of mass politics, we care most not about who posts but about who gets read – and there are plenty of formal and informal barriers that hinder ordinary citizens' ability to reach an audience. Most online content receives no links, attracts no eyeballs, and has minimal political relevance. Again and again, this study finds powerful hierarchies shaping a medium that continues to be celebrated for its openness. This hierarchy is structural, woven into the hyperlinks that make up the Web; it is economic, in the dominance of companies like Google, Yahoo! and Microsoft; and it is social, in the small group of white, highly educated, male, professionals who are vastly overrepresented in online opinion. (ibid: 18–19)

Hindman describes what he calls a 'Googlearchy', a hierarchy of site selection based on the link structure which makes up the Web and which is built into the search engines most used by consumers – such as Google, Yahoo! and Microsoft Search. According to Hindman, PageRank, the ranking algorithm that powers the Google search engine, is typical in that it 'relies largely on the link structure of the Web to achieve its results' (ibid: 40). The consequence is that the results we receive in response to our search through Google will rank most highly those sites which receive the most links from other sites. Effectively, therefore, sites 'are ranked in a popularity contest in which each link is a vote' – hence the democratizing rubric – but also in which 'the votes of popular sites carry more weight' (ibid: 43) as a result of their greater number of links. This in turn generates even more traffic towards the highly ranked sites, as most people don't go past the first page of their search results. The result is a 'winner take all' outcome, in which a handful of sites at the top of the distribution receive more links than all the other sites put together (ibid: 54). Sites with many inbound links (typically, those produced by well-resourced and diversified media conglomerates) are simply the most visible. Further, this pattern is likely to be self-perpetuating:

'heavily linked sites should continue to attract more links, more eyeballs, and more resources with which to improve the site content, while sites with few links remain ignored' (ibid: 55).

This finding has implications for one of the key ideas driving the commercial application of digital optimism: *Wired* journalist, Chris Anderson's (2006) model of the 'long tail'. Anderson's work has been taken up as an argument for today's media industries to benefit from the new capacities provided through the digital media by discarding their traditional model of production, which invests everything in a couple of big megahits, in favour of investing in a multitude of niche products. It is a move from broadcasting to narrowcasting, with the 'long tail' of revenues drawn from many small markets, Anderson predicted, ultimately exceeding the revenues to be made from the traditional mass market. The 'winner take all' logic of online media in fact works against this: 'audiences on the Web', Hindman finds, 'are actually *more* concentrated on the top ten or twenty outlets than are traditional media like newspapers and magazines' (2009: 134, emphasis in original).[10] The smaller sites certainly do attract their users, but in nothing like the numbers needed to justify Anderson's claims. Hindman puts it this way:

> The problem with Anderson and others is that they have distorted the scale of the phenomenon they are examining; they have made the long tail into the entire dog. At least for news and media sites as well as political sites, it is simply not true that the smallest outlets, taken together, get most of the traffic. Not even close. (ibid: 135)

On the other hand, the smallest outlets do attract more visits than what Hindman calls 'the missing middle', where local media organizations are losing out to national sources and where there is very little traffic at all (ibid: 100). Whatever the angle of inspection you want to adopt, Hindman's results challenge the currently popular conceptions of Web 2.0 and its uses. For instance, his data reveal that web-sites for political advocacy and even 'prominent blogs' get only a tiny fraction of the attention that traditional news outlets receive, and that it is older citizens, rather than younger ones, who spend most time on political sites (ibid: 81). So much for a new political order.

I am simplifying quite complex and detailed research here, and thus I am alert to the dangers of misrepresenting it by treating it briefly as a set of conclusions rather than foregrounding its considerable methodological innovations. Those interested should certainly consult Hindman's work directly. I do want to refer to one more area, though, before moving on. Hindman tests the claims that political blogs have expanded the social and ideological diversity of the political mediasphere in the USA, as well as the possibility that blogging and citizen journalism may one day replace 'elite' or 'old' media (2009: 102). He finds that blogs are a small but rapidly growing part of the media environment, but that their claims to represent the views of ordinary citizens are difficult to sustain. For a start, while the blogosphere may be heavily populated, the data on which blogs actually get read reflect the patterns of online concentration noted earlier on: 'the top five blogs' in the United States, 'taken together' he says, 'account for 28 per cent of blog traffic; the top ten blogs accounted for 48 per cent' (ibid: 113). What's more, Hindman also picks up the close association we have noted already in this book – that between bloggers and journalists working in traditional media. Examining the backgrounds of the top ten bloggers in the USA, he finds that five of them are 'current or former journalists from traditional news organizations' (ibid: 116); taking on a larger sample, and widening the definition to include those with backgrounds in public relations, op-ed columns and other journalism-related activities, Hindman's 'census' of bloggers found nearly 'two-fifths claimed close familiarity with traditional reporting, periodical publishing, and opinion journalism' (ibid: 122).

Hindman also notes similarities in the media roles played by the political blogger and the op-ed columnist – an observation that further increases the distance between bloggers and ordinary citizens. The op-ed columnist, after all, is not your ordinary journalist. The op-ed columnist has an elite role within the traditional media: unlike those of most journalists, their opinions are explicit and they matter. According to Hindman, though, they actually constitute a less elite formation than that of the leading bloggers. Hindman's bloggers' census compares the social and educational backgrounds of 30 op-ed columnists from papers such as the *New York Times* and the *Washington Post* with those of the top 30 bloggers. He finds that the op-ed columnists, while certainly constituting a media and political elite, nevertheless as a 'group are in some ways more representative of the public than the top bloggers are' (ibid: 126). The top bloggers are more highly educated, for example (more than half had a PhD), and attend more elite educational institutions. While bloggers might claim to represent the views of ordinary citizens, Hindman's census suggests that this is a bit of a stretch. The leading bloggers are members of a highly-educated political elite, well established within the media industries, and already accustomed to having their voices heard. And, unlike most ordinary citizens, they are, overwhelmingly, white, male professionals. Hindman concludes:

> Given the mythology that still surrounds online politics, it is necessary to emphasize the obvious. The small group of bloggers who receive tens of thousands of hits daily are clearly political elites. Prominent online political groups, such as MoveOn.org, still rely heavily on formal and informal elites to run their organizations. Political candidates and their paid staff members *certainly* qualify as political elites. All of the most celebrated examples of online politics have relied on political elites in order to persuade, coordinate and organize. Moreover, the new Internet elites are not necessarily more representative of the general public than the old elites are. Those claiming that the Internet is democratizing politics need to start by acknowledging these central facts. (ibid: 141, emphasis in original)

What Hindman's research on political blogging suggests to me is that the internet has facilitated the rise of a new aristocracy of opinion, in which certain elite, digitally literate, individuals have been able to make use of digital media to address significantly larger audiences than were previously available to them through traditional media. These may be, in some ways, *new* formations of elites, and one can see how that in itself would be of benefit to a democratic politics. Nonetheless, this is a very different kind of effect to that customarily claimed for politics on the internet. In the United States, there is a liberal bias in the blogosphere which probably maximizes the likely socio-political benefits (that is, it reinforces tolerance of a broad range of competing opinions), and minimizes the possible deficits, to flow from this aristocracy of opinion. However, it is worth remembering that there is nothing inherent in these technologies which privileges the liberal, the tolerant, or the progressive in terms of the opinions they can carry. The establishment of an influential political elite who pointed the other way is, theoretically, just as possible.

There are plenty of examples of precisely this eventuality elsewhere. The rise of the 'shock-blog' in the Netherlands constitutes a very clear parallel to the rise of the shock-jock in US talk radio, where, as we saw in Chapter 4, a highly conservative politics rules. Geert Lovink has written about his return to the Netherlands from Australia in 2004, and his difficulty in reconciling the fact 'that this once liberal, tolerant country was dominated by tough-talking bloggers, whose non-conformist attitude was aimed at breaking the liberal consensus, and who openly expressed racist and anti-Semitic diatribes under the banner of free speech' (2008: 8). Lovink accuses the shock-blogs of playing a significant role in the 'ongoing saga around the murder of Dutch filmmaker Theo Van Gogh' (who himself ran a shock-blog): shock-blogs 'set the tone of the discussion', Lovink says, 'thereby further fuelling tensions between (ethnic) communities' (ibid: 9). As I demonstrated in relation to talk radio in Chapter 4, open access does not guarantee that the media will be used for democratic or even pro-social purposes. Instead, as Lovink puts it: 'blogs are utilized by anyone, for any purpose' (ibid: 9).

This suggests that it is time to broaden the scope of this discussion in order to acknowledge how different such purposes can be, how differently the technologies of digital media can be used, and how different the opportunities of access are, in various national and international contexts – as well as at various socio-economic levels. All of these differences have the potential to trouble the certainties of digital optimism. The introduction to Goggin and McLelland's *Internationalising Internet Studies* (2009) opens with a description of a young Palestinian girl being introduced to the internet by workers with an international aid agency. She has no experience of using a computer, let alone the internet. When she is asked whether she wants English or Arabic script, she admits that she is unable to read at all (ibid: 3). The challenge for those attempting to help this girl starts a lot further back than they had realized. This is a reminder of, among other things, the fact that the enthusiasm for the emancipatory potential of the internet is only enabled by normatizing western affluence, and that it too easily ignores the very different conditions prevailing for most of the rest of the world:

> We must remember to ask who is *not* online, and what are the costs and consequences of this absence. With most of the world's population lacking a stable system of telephony – let alone the provision of broadband – we start to see how the democracy affirmed through Web 2.0 replicates many colonial structures of the nineteenth century. The empowered speak on behalf of the disempowered – the old, the disabled, the black and the poor. Instead of recognising this ventriloquism, the loud affirmation of digital democracy drowns out not only any critique, but any space to hear the silences in this pseudo-utopic discourse. (Brabazon, 2008: 68–9, emphasis in original)

Where such issues are recognized, and fortunately this is happening increasingly as a result of projects such as Goggin and McLelland's and similar developments in media and cultural studies (Curran and Park, 2004; McMillin, 2007; Thissu, 2009), it is important to acknowledge the role played by the political and regulatory contexts. The openness of the internet is not of itself comprehensively constitutive; there are plenty of jurisdictions which have proved capable of regulating access and content on the internet through deals struck with transnational providers as part of the price of entry to their market. China is only the largest of many such countries which have shown that the internet can operate apparently successfully for most of its citizens without necessarily embracing the degrees of openness so prized in the West (Fung, 2008).

The essays collected together in *Internationalising Internet Studies* highlight the specificities and contingencies involved in the take-up and use of digital media around the world. While many in the West continue to see the USA as the model for what is assumed to be an evolutionary process of development, with less developed nations taking their place in an historical queue, Goggin and McLelland point to the very different outcomes produced outside of the West. These are not only the product of the policy framework within specific regulatory jurisdictions such as those of China or Saudi Arabia, they are also, and perhaps more importantly, the product of the broader socio-cultural context from which the internet has emerged in each instance. Goggin and McLelland cite the example of Japan where mobiles, and not personal computers, have led the way in connecting people to the internet; indeed there are further important differences which have shaped the history of the internet within that culture:

> As Mizuko Ito points out, in Japan (and, to an extent, in other Asian societies) mobile communications technologies were not 'conceived by an elite and non-commercial technological priesthood and disseminated to the masses', but emerged out of Japanese consumers' love of 'gadget fetishism and techno-fashion', and the market was driven, not by a business elite, but rather grew out of the existing pager culture of teenage Japanese girls. (2009: 4)

As they go on to say, among the purposes of gathering their collection of essays is their hope of adding 'to the growing recognition that communications technologies with a "global" reach also are situated in very local cultures of use' (ibid: 4).[11] Among these, despite the lead position the American market takes in the rhetoric of digital optimism, the USA is a long way off the pace – with young people's access to the internet there lagging significantly behind that enjoyed by their peers in the Czech Republic, Macao, Canada and the UK (Lawsky, 2008), while their broadband speeds cannot compare with those of South Korea. Indeed, for a variety of reasons which would make an interesting book in itself, Asia is increasingly looking like the region where digital and mobile media are going to make the most distinctive social and cultural impact and from which the leading patterns for the future cultures of consumption and production may emerge. It is not, however, a region in which a democratic politics can be taken for granted.

YouTube, interactivity and free labour

Thus far I have focused both on the bloggers and on those who participate in their online conversations, as well as examining the claims made for the democratizing influence of this kind of interactivity. Yet it is the video aggregators and social networking sites that have been the most publicized developments in recent years, often for the wrong reasons: their use by teenagers tends to generate regular outbreaks of moral panic in the traditional media (Burgess and Green, 2009). Nonetheless, they are where I can find the strongest evidence of new kinds of participatory cultures changing the nature of media consumption.

'We no longer watch films or TV, we watch databases', says Geert Lovink, in the introduction to his co-edited collection of essays on YouTube (Lovink and Neiderer, 2008: 9). It is not hard to see what he means. The process of consumption for YouTube involves the logics of the search rather than those of the narrative, and relies on the visible immanence of connectedness – as the menus for other choices from the database and links to other sites compete for attention. Although YouTube has become one of the reference points for the commentariat's criticism of Generation Y – it is cited as evidence of their short attention span, their capture by the celebrity industries and their, as it were, overall shallowness – it is worth recognizing how wide and varied its pleasures actually are. First, it has added another dimension of experience for the audience of mainstream commercial entertainment. Building on what had always been there in the entertainment press (the daily reporting of newsworthy, 'cool' and embarrassing moments from television, cinema and the popular music industries in particular), YouTube provides direct access to the raw material. During the 2008 American elections, from my home in Australia, instead of merely reading about Tina Fey's impersonation of Sarah Palin on *Saturday Night Live* in the US, I could go onto YouTube and watch it. Not only does this provide us with a dramatic internationalization of popular cultural forms, it also delivers ready access to a repertoire of popular culture texts that may not have been screened on domestic television networks but are nonetheless attractive to significant sections of the audience. (The effects of this are visible in video stores in Australia: rows of DVDs for television shows which are known via YouTube but which have never been screened on television here.) This offers the same 'pleasures of access', the 'metropolitanising buzz' (Turner, 2005: 131) our first contact with international cable channels initially generated; the added benefit is that, in this case, the choices are personal, immediate and, within limits, customizable.

This is a new avenue of access to Nick Couldry's (2003) media centre, and one can understand how it would generate an enhanced sense of power over one's media diet (certainly when compared to the experience of reading the broadcast television schedule), as well as a demonstration of global connectedness in which the user is ahead of the mainstream media circuits (viral networks can alert users to a new 'cool' text well before it winds up being shown on the evening news). It is also exciting because of the sense of co-presence that can accompany the viewing of a popular video online. The experience of co-presence (the imagined presence of a wider community watching with you simultaneously) has been regarded conventionally as among the characteristics of the consumption of broadcast television (Ellis, 2002: 176), where it is usually articulated to the national audience. For a YouTube user, I think there is also an analogous co-presence, not necessarily simultaneous, but framed by transnational taste niches or by social networks rather than by citizenship or geography. As a result, perhaps, there are not only the rewards which come from the personalized and individualized choices, but there is also the possibility of an imagined transnational community.

Second, YouTube's interactive capacities have provided the dominant platform for user-generated content in which DIY productions (or as Jean Burgess carefully puts it, 'ostensibly user-created videos' (2008: 102)) can attract enormous international audiences – Judson Lappley's 'The Evolution of Dance' had pulled in more than 85 million views by May 2008 (ibid: 103). More importantly, for some, a participatory culture (very much smaller, as we have seen, but still significant in terms of the attractions of the site for all of its participants) of user-generated productions – mash-ups, parodies, and so on – has developed very quickly in response to the DIY 'alternative' ethos which surrounds this kind of content. Such an ethos is not new in popular culture, of course, but it has previously been most thoroughly connected with rock music and its associated mythologies of resistance, authenticity and anti-commercialism. As digital technologies have enabled cheaper and more mobile production capacities, the garage band ethos of the alternative musician has been translated across media and taken up by the amateur or 'pro-am' video producer. Their audience is gathered virally – through word of mouth, social networks, and so on – and the scale and speed of that mode of distribution have been truly staggering.[12]

This is due to a third dimension of the YouTube experience, which is its function as a social networking site. Burgess argues that 'for those participants who actively contribute content and engage in cultural conversation around online video, YouTube is in itself a social network site, one in which videos (rather than "friending") are the primary medium of social connection between participants' (2008: 102). She examines the take-up and use of several DIY videos, not in order to trace their achievement of commercial success but to demonstrate that the processes by which they are used are among the constitutive capacities of this media technology. Burgess argues that it is necessary to see these videos 'as mediators of ideas that are taken up in practice within social networks, not as discrete texts that are produced in one place and then are later consumed somewhere else by isolated individuals or unwitting masses':

> These ideas are propagated by being taken up and used in new works, in new ways, and therefore are transformed in each iteration – a 'copy the instructions', rather than 'copy the product' model of replication and variation; and this process takes place within and with reference to particular social networks or subcultures. (ibid: 108)

What this highlights, according to Burgess, is the community of 'vernacular creativity' that has emerged around user-generated video accessed through YouTube.

Although it is correct to describe YouTube as a video aggregator, Burgess is arguing that it would be wrong to see it as merely another platform upon which users can view television – even though that is what most users do. YouTube's real novelty seems to lie most in its hybrid capacities: it combines access to an extraordinary database of short-form material with the capacity for viewers to share their favourite selections via email or through links to other social networking sites such as MySpace, as well as providing such a high level of interactivity that it enables 'produsers' to generate their own content and distribute it through the site. Given all of this, it is not surprising that it has been hailed as an important, and empowering, new development both for the media and audiences.

It is not, however, a social networking site in the way that MySpace or Facebook are. The popularity of these sites has grown so quickly that it is still quite difficult to know what kind of role they will play in the future, or whether, indeed, they will flame out and disappear like virtual reality did. So far, though, they perfectly exemplify a trend that media and cultural studies has been discussing for some years: the shift in the media's primary function from constructing citizens to constructing cultural identities (Hartley, 1999). This has been true of much television in the post-broadcast era, but social networking sites possibly demonstrate it best. The social networking site is about the construction, maintenance and performance of cultural identities. The work that goes into updating a personal presence on these sites is demanding – hence the high numbers of abandoned, unattended or otherwise dead pages – and thus requires a high level of investment in time and creativity. In some cases, sites have become sufficiently populated by subcultural or shared interest groups to have become important for broader, offline, processes of cultural production. The grassroots of the popular music industry, for instance, meets the commercial mainstream on MySpace and maintaining a band's MySpace page is becoming part of the promotional infrastructure of the industry.

In all cases, though, what is notable about the user-generated content on the social networking sites is the level of affective investment required. This is a highly developed technology of the self which enables a customized, endlessly iterative, performance of individual identity. According to Larissa Hjorth's (2008a) study of the social networking site, Cyworld, in South Korea, there are significant differences in the way the technology has been taken up there – to do with a more 'seamless' connection to the offline and local community – but the level of affective investment in 'mediated forms of intimacy' is even greater. A number of her respondents complained about how much time it took to maintain their customized 'mini-hompies' (their personal pages on Cyworld):

> Here, we see the downside to customization by way of the paradox of technology: rather than freeing us, it further enslaves us. Behind the politics of immediacy or fast-forwarding presence

(the perpetual practice of almost immediate representation of offline experiences online) lie actual labor-intensive customization techniques. (2008a: 243)

As with most of the examples of the demotic turn I have dealt with in this book, the problem for cultural and media studies here is not with the practices and modes of participation in themselves; this is not a moralistic or elitist critique of popular culture and I have no interest in declaring any of the media practices upon which I have focused attention as inherently a 'good' or a 'bad' thing. Rather, my overarching concern is with the significance that has been attributed to these practices by academic researchers which, in some cases, misunderstands their functions and, in certain others, amounts to a defence of what I would consider an abuse of media power. In relation to social networking sites, there is certainly reason to regard these as embodying new models for the construction and circulation of identities. Those who use these sites regularly have a major personal investment in them, and draw particular kinds of sustenance from them. To regard them as therefore unproblematically empowering, though, is to overlook the structures which contain them: who owns these constructions of identities, and who benefits from their maintenance.

Relatively early on in the development of user-generated content for the internet, Tiziana Terranova (2000) raised concerns about the politics of the provision of free labour within the digital economy. She addressed herself to a wider field of concerns than I am dealing with here: the expansion of the internet which has supported 'contemporary trends towards increased flexibility of the workforce, continuous reskilling, freelance work, and the diffusion of practices such as "supplementing" (bringing supplementary work home from the conventional office)' (2000: 34). However, Terranova is responding to a similar set of optimistic claims about the liberating potential of the internet: 'the Internet does not automatically turn every user into an active producer, and every worker into a creative subject', she warns (ibid: 35). Furthermore, she is one of the first to focus on what has become a fundamental paradox: the ways in which the putative freedom offered by the internet has persuaded us to set aside some of the basic safeguards that protect us from exploitation. The consequences of this include western cultures' increasing acceptance of consumer surveillance, their disregard for their loss of control over the confidentiality of private information (Andrejevic, 2007), and the collapse of the distinction between work and leisure in particular areas of employment (Gregg, 2008; Ross, 2004). It is the last of these that most concerns Terranova: our agreement to provide our labour free in a transaction through which the 'knowledgeable consumption of culture is translated into productive activities that are pleasurably embraced and at the same time shamelessly exploited' (2000: 37). Nonetheless, and in spite of 'the numerous, more or less disingenuous endorsements of the democratic potential of the Internet', and while 'the links between it and capitalism look a bit too tight for comfort to concerned political minds' (ibid: 38), this remains an implication which the prevailing arguments about the social and political benefits of the internet have continued to overlook.

This is a fundamental issue for our understanding of social networking sites, where the development of the product is accomplished by its users, freely and for pleasure. There is a commercial benefit to the site from this activity and the greater the degree of personal investment in the development of a user's page which the site can encourage, the greater the commercial benefit. Not only does this user-generated content enhance and enrich the site and the brand, it also confirms a user's commitment to this particular site:

> The communities that emerge, the integration of social networking into daily life, and the personal biography you create through your content, comments etc., create an impressively strong tie to a particular site. The demography of the people I interviewed places them on the left side of the political spectrum; they are at times directly anti-corporate/capitalist in the pictures they upload and their comments. Nonetheless, most of them do not see a problem in having such close ties with a particular company. This can only be explained with reference to the immense joy and pleasure they get out of sharing photos online. The huge amount of work that goes into each personal site is paid back in an affective currency: the joy and significance these sites bring to their users. (Petersen, 2008: 8)

These users can't simply take their network with them if they wish to migrate to another social networking site in response to changes in the format or operation of the site. Unpaid content providers in an 'architecture of participation', they can also find themselves trapped within an 'architecture of exploitation and enclosure' (Petersen, 2008: 8).

There has been growing concern about these issues within media and cultural studies, leading to a more contingent view of the benefits of interactivity. In this context, interactivity 'doubles' as a form of labour and has two kinds of products: affective and social benefits for the user, and economic benefits for the host (Andrejevic, 2008: 47). Given the customary equation of interactivity with empowerment, as well as its identification with an individualist, anti-corporate subversiveness (the ideologies running beneath the celebration of the produser), there seems to be an odd blindness in much of the academic literature to the actual nature of the transaction:

> It is one thing to note that viewers derive pleasure and fulfilment from their online activities and quite another to suggest that pleasure is necessarily either empowering for viewers or destabilizing for entrenched forms of corporate control over popular culture. (ibid: 43)

In this case, what is so often represented as subversive or anti-corporate behaviour, the personalization of one's interaction with the media, is actually fundamental to the marketing strategies of the corporation. Andrejevic argues that the success in masking the corporate interests involved has become one of the 'defining characteristics of the contemporary deployment of interactivity': 'the ability to enfold forms of effort and creativity previously relegated to relatively unproductive (economically speaking) realms within the digital embrace of the social factory' (ibid: 42). As a result, he suggests, we need to dispense with the familiar, and still relatively uncontested, binary in cultural studies that opposes the consumer's 'complicit passivity' to the user's 'subversive participation'. Andrejevic tells us it is just not that simple.

In a similar vein, Kylie Jarrett (in an article entitled 'Interactivity is Evil!'), while recognizing the flexibilities enabled by social networks (and indeed, by Web 2.0 in general) as well as the control available to users in determining how they interact with them, signals her neo-Foucauldian position by locating her critique of these interactions under the sharply appropriate subheading of 'Discipline and Seduce'. She foregrounds social networking sites' 'masking of power in order to effect control' and describes interactivity as a 'disciplining technology' with a particular effect:

> It is assuredly not a disciplining into regimented control such as that effected upon and within the soldiers of Foucault's account, but it is a disciplining into a liberal ideal of subjectivity based around notions of freedom, choice and activity. This discipline is not about the construction of 'docile bodies', yet it remains true to the spirit through which this is achieved – the normalisation and inculcation of subjection to power. The active, self-governing subjects who are addressed and produced in Web 2.0 are no less a product of discipline than prisoners in the Panopticon or soldiers in their regimented drill practice. (2008b: 8)

The reference to the Panopticon may seem a little extreme in this context, but it would be remiss of me to leave this part of the discussion without picking up on the connection with the idea of surveillance by pointing out that 'user-generated content' does not only include comments, videos and profiles; it also includes the data consumers provide both to government and to commercial monitoring and marketing organizations as a product of their online interactions. That, too, has attracted attention from those who see the expansion of this activity as dangerous rather than emancipatory, and has generated debate and further research on the monitoring and surveillance of online behaviour (see, for example, Andrejevic, 2007).

Conclusion

The political implications of interactivity, then, are still up for debate. Indeed, we are probably witnessing the beginnings of a revision of the orthodox rhetorics of empowerment, enforcing the recognition of the contradictions inherent in many of the transactions which result in user-generated content online. However, there seems to be no doubt that there are new forms of participation available to consumers online and it is not at all surprising that, for those who still wish to chart the signs of the reclamation of consumer sovereignty within the mediascape, user-generated content is the lead contender. There are lots of reasons to take such a view.

As we have seen, though, participation is turning out to be a slightly more complicated notion than originally thought. There are issues to do with who participates, and how their access is enabled. There are competing views on whether those who participate by contributing content are involved in a creative act or whether they are unwittingly donating their labour to a commercial interest or, indeed, whether they are doing both. The egalitarian, anti-corporate ethic which drives much of the celebration of the political potential of Web 2.0 sits uncomfortably with the fact that their enthusiasms are supporting interests that are nonetheless, uncontestably, commercial. As Terranova put it, the links between the digital optimists and the interests of capital are 'too tight for comfort'. There is also another range of issues to do with the blurring of the difference between serving the public good and serving a commercial interest; this can take the form of a debate about whether a service such as Facebook is directed towards the construction of a community, or towards the promotion of a product – or, indeed, whether in practice that actually matters. And there is another debate over what actually constitutes participation anyway: is it the 1 per cent who contribute DIY content, or is it 'all those who upload, view, comment on or create content' (Burgess and Green, 2009: 57)?

There has been a second thread running through this chapter that I want to revisit in this concluding section. The problems I have been dealing with have their roots in the claims for the importance of Web 2.0 that I am suggesting have pushed academic discussion past the point of disinterested analysis and into the area of media activism. The projected benefits for 'ordinary people' have created an understandable enthusiasm, but this seems to have resulted in a loss of perspective and proportion in the assessment of what has actually been achieved. Jean Burgess has suggested to me, in a personal response to an early version of this chapter, that there could be a more positive way of viewing such a failing than I have so far allowed. That is, that the utopian character of so much of this work could be understood more appropriately as an aspirational claim on the future rather than an empirical claim on the present. While such work may appear to be complicit with the media industries, she has argued, there is also the possibility that their boosting of the potential of a more participatory media is part of a legitimate attempt to persuade the mainstream media to take on such a model. I can see how that might well be the case and that this would certainly moderate the kinds of criticisms I have made in this discussion.

Nonetheless, I have no doubt that a more modest and evidence-based set of claims for the cultural and industrial effects of Web 2.0 would enable a more realistic understanding of what is currently the case, as well as providing the basis for properly thinking through cultural and media policy issues for the future. A greater acknowledgement of the lessons from media history would help as well. There really hasn't been much of an historical dimension to the cultural and media studies accounts of new media – despite the fact that each new development is usually described as if it is of historic proportions. It might be unkind to say this, but on the current evidence it looks like the digital optimists would actually be the last to know if there were significant historical continuities between developments in new media and those which had preceded them. For some reason, it has become almost obligatory to emphasize the disruptive and discontinuous character of new media without so much as a backwards glance.

We have reason to be concerned about the motivated nature of so much of this analysis, as well as the unrealistic promises that have been extracted from it:

> Despite all the talk, the Internet has not delivered the revolution it promised. Societies adapt to Information and Communication Technologies (ICTs) but do not change in a fundamental way and prove remarkably flexible in staying as they are ... How can libertarian techno-celebrities continue to sell dream worlds about freedom and levelling the fields without being scrutinized? There is little indication that they will shut up or even face serious opposition. There seems to be a never-ending demand among geeks and entrepreneurs for salvation. We can only repeat so often that the Web is not a place apart. (Lovink, 2008: xxvi–xxvii)

Geert Lovink's exasperation here is focused on the self-interest to which he attributes the 'libertarian techno-celebrities'' boosting of the political potential of the Web. While I would acknowledge that issue as well, my primary concern is more to do with the erosion of academic distance and disciplined protocols of analysis in the way that these academics (some of whom may be the techno-celebrities Lovink has in mind) have dealt with such developments.

In their enthusiasm to present their work to a public who might actually respond, many academics have established blogs and many have argued that this is an activity which is fundamental to their professional mission. On the face of it, that is an important and useful function for the academic, particularly in our fields. It is difficult in that context, though, to maintain the distinctions between academic research and public commentary. The forms of expertise and authority involved in writing one's blog and writing an academic article are not the same, but at times their differences are elided. So, when Henry Jenkins (2008) uses his blog to celebrate the value of 'just-in-time scholarship' – the timely and immediate contributions academics can make to public debate through their blogs – this looks to me, on balance, like an overvaluing of the publication of opinion and an undervaluing of the protocols of academic research.

As is the case with commentary on Web 2.0 in general, the academic treatment of participatory media and user-generated content has also been inordinately preoccupied with predicting the future. Often without the support of empirical data or accounting for historical trends in the relevant locations, digital optimists move into futurologist mode at the drop of a hat. It is not enough to note the rise of user-generated content online; one has to predict where it will end up, which technologies will rise or fall, and what media formations will disappear. Some of this, as we noted earlier, draws conclusions that, on the available evidence, are not supportable or make predictions that are simply unrealistic. Anyone attempting to see into the future would need to recognize that there must be limits to the pattern of fragmentation and individualization that has been so important in driving the online production and consumption of media, but which is so antipathetic to the more traditional media models which, we need to remember, still control the global media economy. History tells us, also, that the predictions coming from early adopters are notoriously poor indicators of how new media technologies will actually be taken up. There is more than simple arithmetic involved here. We are going to require a lot more than the aggregation of a bunch of figures (often, themselves of dubious validity because of their commercial origin) noting the rise and fall of audiences and the take-up of various technologies.

There are, of course, examples of academic research which do rise to this challenge, and I want to close this chapter by referring to an example from the so-called 'digital storytelling' movement. Digital storytelling is a 'workshop-based practice in which people are taught to use digital media to create short audio-video stories, usually about their own lives'. Developed by the late Dana Atchley, this project set out to put some flesh on the bones of the egalitarian promise of the digital era by teaching ordinary people – 'from school students to the elderly, with or (usually) without knowledge of computers or media production' – how to produce their own personal video (Hartley and McWilliam, 2009a: 3). Unlike some of the developments I have been dealing with in this book, it is comparatively (though not entirely, it must be admitted) free of exaggerated claims for its significance. Its crucial attribute, though, is that it has provided a direct and practical response 'to the exclusion of "ordinary" people's stories in broadcast media' (ibid: 4). This has been made possible by developments in digital media – digital cameras, scanners, digital home media – becoming increasingly accessible, not just in the home but also through public facilities such as libraries. Significantly, and as we have seen, while the commercial nature of so much of what drives Web 2.0 raises worrying contradictions, digital storytelling seems to have been largely a public sector initiative so far, typically involving educational institutions, community organizations, cultural institutions and other hosts such as public broadcasters, health groups and churches (McWilliam, 2009: 39). This may be a crucial factor in the kinds of successes it can report and in the 'public good' outcomes it can produce. Digital storytelling has a significant presence online and Kelly McWilliam (2009) has written up the results of an international survey of 300 programmes operating around the world.

There are many research projects described in Hartley and McWilliam's collection of essays, *Story Circle: Digital Storytelling Around the World*, but I want to note just one. Jo Tacchi's project, called 'Finding a Voice', is 'a multi-sited ethnographic study of – and experiment in – local participatory content creation involving a network of local media initiatives in India, Nepal, Sri Lanka and Indonesia' (Tacchi, 2009: 168). The project's aim is to investigate how digital media technologies can be most 'effective and empowering in each local context', and specifically how it can 'empower poor people to communicate their "voices" within and beyond marginalised communities' (ibid: 169). What Tacchi means by 'voices' is not simply the ability to utter sounds. Rather, it refers to people's 'inclusion and participation in social, political and economic processes, meaning making, autonomy and expression' (ibid.). This, then, is aimed precisely at getting 'voices' *heard*. Tacchi reports that digital storytelling has provided an ideal means of promoting the participation of marginalized communities in this instance, notwithstanding what she describes as the 'messiness and problematic natures of both "participation" and "development", and most certainly of "participatory development"' (ibid.) within the contexts in which her work took place. I am not going to deal here with what this 'messiness' involved; we have already canvassed a number of the issues which complicate these terms, but the approach does seem to be iterative and negotiated, as well as bottom-up. This is not a bunch of outsiders parachuting in to tell the locals what they need. Rather, it is a long-term, institutionally-based and careful process of listening for ways that can enable the locals to participate in the decision making which will drive their own media development.

This demonstrates a more sophisticated understanding of the cultural politics of digital media than the simple equation of access with empowerment, or of the popular with the democratic, even though it is still driven by the same kind of ideals that motivate the work of the digital optimists. Its usefulness lies in the fact that it is a good example of what grounded, long-term research projects might actually achieve – and not only in the 'development' context of this project.

There is nothing revolutionary about digital storytelling, and its achievements are likely to be both modest and local, but for my purposes its importance lies in the fact that it does seem as if its programme of specific interventions demonstrates how academic work might assist in developing the capacities needed to deliver convincingly on the democratizing promise of digital media.

Notes

1 I have only heard this term used once, by a 'social network analyst' on a radio programme discussing blogging. I'll admit to being a little staggered at the presumption of the term, with its significant pre-empting of history.

2 Or, alternatively, for collectors of neologisms, 'prosumer'.

3 While some formulations of these terms are quite precise and involve relatively advanced technical knowledge, I am using this here in its broadest possible application to refer to those who participate online through the provision of user-generated content.

4 It is worth noting how, secreted in this title, we can find the residues of the fear of government and the state I mentioned in Chapter 4 as one of the peculiarly American features of conservative thought.

5 I am indebted to my colleague Melissa Gregg for drawing this to my attention.

6 For instance, Axel Bruns's recent article (2008b) on 'produserage' makes a number of citations to Mark Pesce's (2006) blog, which itself cites very little evidence at all (there is the occasional link to other sites, videos, and so on, but virtually no use of verifiable or authoritative sources). In one example, Bruns cites Pesce's refutation of what Pesce calls 'the Big Lie of Big Media', which is that 'if it isn't professionally produced, the audience won't watch it' (Bruns, 2008b: 84) – an argument advanced in order to question the long-term commercial viability of pro-am, amateur or DIY video. The comment comes from Pesce's blog, where there is no evidence to support it. Yet the opinion definitely needs some support if we are going to take it seriously, since all the research I have found agrees that, on balance, professionally produced content 'continues to dominate as the primary source where people get their news and media' (Manovich, 2008: 34).

7 It also overestimates the capacities of the blogger's format. The need for immediacy, brevity and a clear opinion that marks so much of blogging necessarily works against the incorporation of thorough academic research or investigative journalism (Lovink,

2008: 38), and therefore against the kind of expectations we might have of their authority and credibility.

8 Television viewing in the UK also increased by a small percentage over 2008.

9 The methodology is indeed complex, involving technical expertise I don't have, so readers are directed towards the appendix in Hindman's (2009) book which outlines the research approach in detail.

10 While this research is dealing with news and political sites, a similar pattern can be observed across entertainment sites. The boom in watching online video, for instance, is highly concentrated as well. Nielsen Online's Video Census for October 2008 reports that YouTube attracted a total of 5,077,720 video streams for the month, while the next most popular site, Fox Interactive, attracted 244,246 (Nielsen Wire, 2008). The internet has a habit of creating winners who obliterate competition – think Amazon.com, for instance, or eBay – rather than expanding possibilities.

11 Examples include Larissa Hjorth's books on mobile technologies (2008b) and gaming (2009) in the Asia Pacific.

12 Although it probably needs to be said that there are still limitations to the commercialization or 'monetization' of this mode of distribution, it doesn't (yet, in my view) provide support for Anderson's logic of the 'long tail'.

6

The Entertainment Age: the media and consumption today

The entertainment age

We have become accustomed to the routine application of the phrase, the 'information society', to describe the current era (even though the origins of the phrase can be traced back to at least the 1920s). We are also told that we are living in an 'information age', in which our access to information is unprecedented, and accelerating, as it drives social, organizational and economic change. The related claim that we are also living in a digitally-driven 'network society' (Castells, 2000) is also familiar, and these days rarely problematized when the concept crops up in mainstream journalism, public policy documents, and cultural and economic commentary. At the most literal and experiential level, there is every reason why these should be persuasive ideas: most of the western world has 24-hour news services on its television, its citizens can read as many newspapers as they like online; their search engines can dredge up the most arcane information and deliver it in seconds; whole books can be accessed via the internet; mobile phones can receive sports updates, messages, attachments and emails; social networking is the fastest-growing user activity on the Web; email has colonized the practices of professional life; and Wikipedia has become a collaborative information-sharing exercise that makes the conventional encyclopedia look like a steam engine.

I am not interested in contesting the idea of the information society here, but I certainly want to complicate it by highlighting a development that exerts a significant influence in a different direction. One of the fundamental factors in the 'rise of opinion' I highlighted in my account of the redefinition of journalism in Chapters 3 and 4 has been the way that the media industries have embraced the commercial strategy of turning information into entertainment.

Within such a process, at its most pronounced, the traditional 'objective' news format gives way to FOX News, where the brandishing of opinion serves as a means of attracting notoriety, controversy and audiences. To some extent, of course, and not to overstate the situation, such a strategy has always been there – we have had 'weather girls' bringing us the weather reports and retired sports stars providing 'colour' commentary for live sports, as well as a fully developed presentational aesthetic used to design the look of television news programmes. My argument, however, is that this is now a more pervasive and a more structural factor than ever before, with the capacity to challenge our views on the comprehensiveness or even the appositeness of labels such as the information society. The developments I have in mind here include those discussed in Chapter 3 – talk radio, blogging, the entertainment orientation of the web-sites for major news organizations – as well as the massive expansion in entertainment content generated by multi-channel environments for television and the burgeoning market for online video. Indeed, you could argue that the trend is exemplified by what has happened to our use of the home computer. Once seen as an information, education and organizational tool, its primary use is now for entertainment; in fact, it has been reported that some sections of the US audience (the so-called 'millennials', or 14–25 year olds), now regard the computer as a more central entertainment device than their television (Deloitte, 2009).

I am far from the only person to have observed this trend, of course. The term 'infotainment' was coined by the television industry many years ago to describe precisely the kinds of products to which I refer. The provenance I attribute to the current iteration of the trend goes further than this neologism allows, however; more than a strategic shift in genre or format, it also constitutes a shift in function and purpose. Theodore Hamm quotes *New York Times* columnist Nicholas Kristof as complaining that 'one medium after another has found it profitable to turn from information to entertainment, from nuance to table-thumping'. Arguing that this trend had been pioneered by talk radio, Kristof goes on to trace its influence on cable news, political books, internet debates and, finally, documentary cinema (Hamm, 2008: 64). (His specific target at the time was the latest film from Michael Moore.) It would be hard to argue with these claims, even though one might want to question the point of view that motivates their being advanced in the first place. Conventionally, of course, and this is so in Kristof's case, declaiming the rising hegemony of entertainment is a standard strategy within elite critiques of the media and popular culture in general. It is important to stress that this is not my objective here. I am not setting out to deplore this development *en bloc* – even though there are specific aspects of its performance which I have criticized over the course of this book. Rather, my objective is to make a claim for a need to recognize the importance of the role that entertainment has come to play in our patterns of media consumption today, as well as its structural centrality to the part that the media now play, more generally, in our culture.

It is also important, when considering the role of the media in the information society, to recognize the continuing centrality of pleasure to any account of ordinary people's engagement with the media – something that tends to be elided in accounts of the media which focus on the provision of information. Information is simply not enough. Instead, entertainment has become the most pervasive discursive domain in twenty-first-century popular culture, colonizing 'people's identities and imaginations' (Manovich, 2008: 36). Manovich points out that even supposedly subversive user-generated content online 'either directly follows the templates and conventions set by [the] professional entertainment industry, or directly re-uses professionally produced content (for instance, anime music videos)' (ibid: 36). Virtually all the formats and genres that I have dealt with in this book, and that have incorporated the participation of the ordinary citizen, turn information into entertainment in one way or another. It is not a surprising choice, of course, as those media producers who have not taken that route have found life difficult. Traditional news and current affairs programmes on television are in decline in a number of markets, and many newspapers are finding it hard to survive as primarily a mass-market print medium; in the United States and Australia, commercial radio current affairs has virtually disappeared. The information society might still be hungry for information, and may be even more focused on its social networks than ever, but it seems to have had enough of information as a presentational format. Now people want their information sorted for them by talk radio hosts, arranged as a personalized menu on video aggregators' web-sites, structured by the soap opera narratives of reality TV, or processed into a series of spectacular stunts by activist documentary makers like Michael Moore. And, mostly, in the developed world at least, that is how they get it.

What has reinforced this trend, or perhaps even instigated it, is the overwhelming commercialization of the media as entertainment industries. Originally, many countries, particularly those in Europe, had developed communications systems which contained a mix of public and commercial media; now, most of these have withdrawn from investing in publicly-funded media and have allowed the market to rule. As the battle for market success has unfolded, it has become clear that the central commercial focus must rest upon the provision of entertainment; even where information is provided, such as via news services or lifestyle programming, it is wrapped in the packaging of entertainment in order to attract significant audiences. That doesn't, I should add here, simply or necessarily equate to a 'dumbing down' of the media – again, the kind of argument which might conventionally accompany such an observation. It is important to recognize that the trade between information and entertainment does not proceed in one direction alone and that entertainment and information are not mutually exclusive categories. I cited the example of Michael Moore earlier on, and it is worth noting that his capacity to make a strongly argued political documentary entertaining resulted in many people who had never gone to a cinema to see a documentary before, doing so for the first time to see *Fahrenheit 911*.[1] The case has also been argued, in relation to the rise of the hybrid news and entertainment formats, exemplified by *The Daily Show* in the USA but existing in many variations around the world, that these programmes are not only generating the pleasures of entertainment but are also broadening a national conversation about politics by attracting an audience whose members had largely lost their connection with traditional news and current affairs – or, to put it another way, that were no longer being effectively addressed by these services.

There are at least two sides to the narrative we might construct in describing what I am calling here the 'entertainment age'. On the one hand, we have a massive expansion in the provision of content, of cultural productions of all kinds, accessible to a gradually increasing proportion of the world's population. This has to be recognized as an extraordinarily rich media environment that has the capacity to inject new possibilities of cultural consumption into our everyday lives. On the other hand, the fact that what makes up this rich media environment is so thoroughly driven by commercial imperatives means, first of all, that it is tightly focused upon matching the competition: history tells us that the outcome of such an orientation is not usually a greater variety or diversity of content. Second, there is no reason to see this competitive environment as necessarily serving any broader, community or national, interests. Rather, the media have their *own* interests, commercial rather than social or cultural, and this is becoming increasingly the case, and increasingly relevant, as time goes on. There is now a new, and generally accepted, rationale for its existence.

One would think that the patterns of participation and consumption set up by the demotic turn, patterns that explicitly seek to satisfy individual preferences and the desire for personalization and customization, would skew the power relations involved towards the interests of the audience and away from the corporation or the state. This is certainly a claim we have encountered repeatedly in this book, and there are indeed some instances where it has occurred. Overall, however, I have argued that this is not at all a necessary or even a likely consequence of the entertainment age. As we have seen already, it would be naïve to regard the rise of the commercial media, in all their various locations, as simply and uncomplicatedly a liberalizing force that will ultimately serve the interests of an audience. In Singapore, or China, for instance, there is reason to argue that the personalized and individualized identities now on offer through increased media choices (access to online social networking sites, video aggregators, blogging, and all the other accoutrements of the digital era) remain nonetheless tightly articulated to the construction and renovation of national identities authorized and promulgated by the state. Zala Volcic's (2009) discussion of the 'commercial nationalism' of the entertainment media in the new nation-states emerging from the former Yugoslavia also discusses this kind of situation.

An audience's new freedoms in such locations, the result of relaxed constraints upon the consumption of entertainment rather than upon the nature of their participation in cultural politics or the economy generally, have proven to be relatively easily incorporated into the service of the state. Indeed, in China, and this may be true of a number of other countries (Saudi Arabia, for instance), the expanded provision of entertainment choices has become a kind of soft power that has delivered liberalization at the cultural level, thus placating the middle-class and urban elites, but without enabling change in the access to power at the political level. Rather than consumer choice presenting a challenge to political control in such locations, it could be argued, it has become an enabling (or consoling) device for the state: the citizen is offered the pleasures of consumption as a surrogate for more substantive political liberalization (Chua, 2000; Sun and Zhao, 2009).

It would be a mistake to see this as simply a feature of more authoritarian societies. In much of the West, the transaction may be more complicated, perhaps, but the 'bread and circuses' implications of the likely political function of the choices offered to consumers in the entertainment age are hard to avoid. In both contexts, the provision of these choices must function as a form of depoliticization: in one context, perhaps, as a tool deliberately used to that end; in another, as a by-product, perhaps, of a more careless but nonetheless effective use of commercial power. It is hard therefore not to see the rise of entertainment as directly implicated in producing the disengagement from the political upon which Couldry et al.'s recent (2007) research has focused, and ultimately, as what Ghassan Hage, following Bourdieu, has described as 'the decline of society'. As we witness a decline in the 'state's commitment to a national society *tout court*' (Hage, 2003: 18), we find, expanding to fill that vacant space, the promise of increased consumer sovereignty over regimes of consumption.

Taking the 'mass' out of mass media

There are limits to both the provision and the exercise of consumer choice, of course, and the commercial media's generation of more and more platforms and products is not likely to continue uninterrupted in a steadily ascending trajectory. On the supply side, the commercial production of entertainment costs money that must be earned, one way or another, from audiences. The economics of this situation have resulted in a significant increase in consumer investment in entertainment hardware, software and content. Most of what has occurred as a consequence of the entertainment age has cost consumers money. Typically, services for which there is a charge are displacing services which were previously delivered free – subscription is replacing broadcast television, for instance. Amanda Lotz cites alarming figures about the proportion of US families' household income being spent on entertainment. She quotes a press report which says that in 2005 the average American spent more on entertainment than on gasoline, household furnishings and clothing, while the wealthiest Americans spent more on entertainment than on health care, utilities, clothing or food eaten in the home (Lotz, 2007: 250)! Perhaps, under the conditions of the global financial crisis that are emerging as I write, we are about to encounter the upper limits to this trajectory.

The context for these shifts in the structure and rationale for the media industries is already one of significant change: it is marked by fragmenting, globalizing and deregulating markets for media products, increased competition for smaller or niche audiences, and, most importantly, in some of the larger domestic markets, the decline of sections of the mass audience – especially for broadcasting. The influence generated by the development and application of digital technologies has been profound – affecting the industrial logics of reproduction, distribution and marketing, as well as enabling a demotic turn towards new practices of consumption, participation and production through social networking and user-generated content. These changes have significantly complicated what seems in retrospect to have been a relatively simple traditional paradigm of mass communication: that is, a communication system focused on institutions or organizations more or less closely articulated to the operation of the state, freely accessible to all, concerned with the production of the citizen as a national subject, and taking as their potential audience the whole of the population of the nation-state.

This paradigm has not disappeared, of course, and in many places it is still well and truly in place. But its universality or comprehensiveness, as well as its function and rationale, are varying and changing. The media are losing their 'massness' – the fundamental assumption that they are aimed at the largest possible audience all of the time. This has significant consequences. Once the media lose their dependence on a mass audience, they are free to act in ways that are more volatile and contingent, as they respond to the precise configuration of the forces of change in particular socio-historical and economic circumstances. Future accounts of the media will need to be especially cognizant of that enhanced volatility in their understandings of what is going on at any one point in time.

Amanda Lotz raises a similar point but in a slightly different way, by framing our understanding of the changing function of the media as a central conceptual question for the field of media studies. The changes which have shaped the multi-channel environment for television, she says, obviously have 'manifold consequences' for the study of the media and their role in society. However, so far, she argues (and I would agree), the focus has been much more on mapping the technological and market shifts rather than on these broader questions – such as 'the significance and repercussions of the erosion of the mass media, or how audiences exercising choice and control require us to revise fundamental ideas about media and culture':

> Questions such as how cultures and subcultures come to know themselves and each other without widely shared programming and how this affects perceptions of difference in society require new thinking. Many assumptions of the 'mass' nature of media undergird theories postulating the emancipatory potential of media. Even as the new norm of niche audiences eliminates some of these imagined possibilities, it may create others. (Lotz, 2007: 247)

We need to rethink further the role of digital media, then, and not just track the shifts and permutations, but instead understand what it might do, and how it will do it. This is related, as Lotz suggests, to those broader questions raised above. If the media are no longer always the 'mass' media, if they no longer gather a heterogeneous national audience into a community in the traditional ways once associated, say, with broadcasting or the national newspaper, then what kinds of broad community function *can* they perform?

There is value in such questions: if television, for instance, once provided a means through which the domestic space was centralized, culturally, and articulated to a nationalized narrative of modernity and progress, what happens to such narratives when the contemporary media emphasize dispersion, mobility and the personal/individual, while articulating the audience to a global entertainment industry or regime of consumption? What are the broader changes to the way we think about our cultural identities in a context like that?

The point to be made here is that as the media become more volatile in the way suggested here, and as they become more thoroughly, organizationally and commercially, invested in entertainment, they lose contact with what has variously been thought of as their fourth estate role, their function as national institutions, their centrality to the operation of the public sphere, and, effectively, their social or community responsibilities. Indeed, there are a number of illustrative cases where the media's central function as entertainment is proffered as a means of excusing media practitioners from acknowledging any social responsibilities. In Australia, during the 'Cash for Comment' controversy of the late 1990s, where talkback radio announcers were accused of taking secret kickbacks from advertisers for presenting their interests in a positive, but apparently independent, manner, one announcer responded to criticism of his ethics by reminding everyone that he was 'an entertainer, not a journalist' (Turner, 2003). In the UK, *Sunday Sport*, a classic 1980s-style tabloid newspaper notorious for printing bogus but entertaining stories ('Aliens Stole My Husband!', that kind of thing), described itself on the masthead as a 'news entertainment', thus establishing the paper's distance from the ethical constraints of journalism, but not its format.

To a greater or lesser extent, then, and depending on the circumstances, the media today are able to divest themselves of the responsibilities of a provider of information to the citizenry, and consequently can see themselves as commercial entities responsible to their shareholders rather than to the community or the nation. Mostly, and certainly in the West, that is how the media are seen now by governments as well. Nonetheless, these shifts in what used to be regarded as the media's social function have not reduced their social, political and cultural centrality. Indeed, as I have outlined in the preceding chapters, in some ways and in spite of themselves, the media have taken on an even more active cultural role in their production of identities. What has declined is the media's acknowledgement that they are, in some way, accountable to the community and, conversely, what has also declined is the power of those regulatory structures which might enable the community to call the media to account.

Some of us might wonder how we got to this point. Couldry et al. ask, rhetorically, 'Why should it not be normal for citizens to have the opportunity to attend public fora – not just in central locations but relatively near to where they live – to communicate to media professionals their views about how media professionals present public life?' 'Why should it not be normal', they go on, for 'media professionals to be seen to be accountable to such fora, and not just to their shareholders, advertisers, and … the licence-payer?' We know, of course, that this is *not* normal, even though Couldry et al. argue that 'if media organizations are … vital to the fabric of democracy, then *all of them* need to be accountable to citizens as directly as other democratic institutions' (Couldry et al., 2007: 194, emphasis in original). While I certainly support such a principle, we are clearly a long way from establishing the mechanisms that would ensure its operation.

Earlier in this book I described the media as working 'like an ideological system without an ideological project'. What I meant by that is that the media still have their ideological effects – such as the production of identities – but that these are produced in a contingent rather than a strategic or institutionally directed manner. As Lila Abu-Lughod puts it in relation to the global patterns in television she has noted through her work in Egypt, television is now a 'commercial medium … which, without a masterplan of purpose' 'glorifies the pleasures and freedoms of consumer choices in defense of the virtues of private life and material ambition' (2005: 193). While it is certainly tempting, and indeed common, to discern some kind of overarching conspiratorial plan in the media's activities, I am more convinced by those accounts which focus on the centrality of their commercial motivations and thus the pure instrumentality of the social, political and cultural effects that are the consequence (intended or otherwise) of commercial decisions. Zala Volcic's account of the 'commercial nationalism' exploited by Balkan television in the service of inventing national identities for the new nation-states to have emerged from the former

Yugoslavia, focuses on the instrumental character of the nationalist entertainments she describes as dominating Balkan television's local content. She gives the example of a popular talk show's treatment of a public debate about the construction of the first mosque to be established in Slovenia (a predominantly Catholic country); the show, she says, 'worked hard to reinforce nationalist prejudices by appealing to religious and ethnic anxieties':

> This is perhaps a classic example of how commercial nationalism functions: since the goal is not political or ideological per se – to foster a sense of class unity, for example, or to rally the nation around a set of political reforms – but purely economic, pre-existing prejudices are exploited rather than challenged. If one might fault state broadcasting for narrowing down the discourse by ruling out opposing viewpoints, commercial nationalism achieves a similar goal through different means. It limits the discourse by playing to dominant sets of prejudices, reproducing and amplifying them – not because of a fear of political reprisals, but rather out of a concern that any such challenge might threaten ratings. (2009: 122)

One could present a similar account as a means of explaining the commercial rationale behind FOX News or talk radio's shock-jocks.

Contingent though these specific strategies might be, the media cannot claim to be innocent of their cultural influence. As we saw earlier in our discussion of *Akademi Fantasia*, the fact that these are 'mere entertainments' does not rob them of their power to frame cultural identities and to feed into social discourses that shape a society's view of itself. Toby Miller reminds us of the media's capacity to 'makeover' reality through representation by looking at that staple of media criticism: the over-representation of certain kinds of media content and the consequent distortion of people's perception of what is happening in their communities:

> Even when crime rates plunge, media discourse about crime rises: as the number of murders declines, press attention to them does the opposite. Similarly, school drug use may diminish, but audiences believe that it increases. The classic case of such absurdities is the popular rhetoric about young African-American men. Rates of violence, homicide, and drug use have fallen dramatically amongst black men under age 30 in

the past decade, but media panic about their conduct has headed in the opposite direction. (2008: 35)

Here, a standard media practice aimed at generating audience interest (the sensationalist over-reporting of crime) has its social by-product: an inaccurate perception of the likely risks to personal safety. As we have seen in the discussion of reality TV in Chapter 2, media representations can affect fundamental aspects of every-day life, and can be all the more pervasive because they are also so mundane.

If we are to take up Amanda Lotz's challenge and ask how the current trends I have been isolating – the erosion of the mass media, the fragmentation of markets, the influence of digital tech-nologies, and the changing roles of the audience – are forcing us to 'revise' our 'fundamental ideas about media and culture', what might we say? One thing is clear, the outcome of such a revision is likely to be far more complicated than the ideas it replaces. As we have seen throughout this book, the attribution of large fundamen-tal shifts is fraught with the dangers of overlooking competing examples and of generalizing from too narrow an evidentiary base.

That said, the role of the media as an institution does seem to be changing so much and in so many locations, that the older, tradi-tional, accounts do need to be modified. For a start, we can say that the institutional model of the media has given way to a more thor-oughly commercial and industrial model; that, in many instances, the idea of a national media is giving way to a more conjunctural blend of national, transnational and sometimes even local forma-tions; and that the media audience is mutating from the model of receptiveness we might identify with broadcasting, towards a range of more active and more demotic modes of participation that vary from the personalized menu model of the YouTube user to the content creation activities of the cit-izen journalist or the blogger. As I have argued in this book, some of these modes of participation are politically empowering, and some are not; and working out the difference between them has to be done in a more specific way than most of the synoptic accounts have done so far.

The role of entertainment is now dominant – for the industry and for its users – and new developments and initiatives will reflect that. Within the media industries themselves, the rapid take-up of new products and new technologies at present seems to be fuelled by something close to panic; even though each new gizmo is greeted with great enthusiasm and hailed as the next 'killer app', most of them have not yet revealed how these can be made to turn a profit. Or, in the jargon of the industry, while there are many new applications for new technologies in the market-place (mostly for online and mobile formats), the difficulty remains of working out how to 'monetize' them. In terms of media content, probably the least crucial area in some way, I would agree with those who have argued that the media have become increasingly engaged in the production of identities, and that the kinds of opportunities they provide towards that end are more and more aimed at the customization and individualization of the experience of consumption. And, finally, while there is great enthusiasm for the potential of social networking, there is no answer to the question of how it might play a part in the much larger process to which Amanda Lotz refers, of 'how cultures and subcultures come to know themselves and each other without widely shared programming' (2007: 247). At present, it seems more likely that this dimension of the traditional mass-media remit will survive, in one way or another, and thus retain what remains the distinctive and probably indispensable attribute of broadcasting – its simultaneous collection of an audience of co-present citizens.

The question of how democratic the demotic turn might be, in the end, is not a question that can be answered in terms of an intrinsic pattern common to all media in all situations. While John Hartley can usefully coin a neologism such as 'democratain-ment' as a means of specifying a form of media participation where 'DIY' entertainment serves democratic purposes, Sun and Zhao (2009: 100) have their own neologism ('indoctritainment') to describe the use of entertainment as a means of reinforcing the moral and political values of the state, specifically in the People's Republic of China. There is evidence that both of these practices thrive in their various contexts – and by that I mean both are genuinely successful forms of popular culture which attract freely choosing, loyal, and engaged, audiences. Addressing the democratizing question from another perspective, and again one that has received much attention in this book, greater audience participation in the production of media content does seem to be a directly contributing factor to what I have described as the rise of opinion. On the one hand, this constitutes an expansion of the public sphere and potentially of the variety of points of view accessible through the media; on the other hand, if this also constitutes the construction of new kinds of elites, even as a product of highly participatory media formations, then the demotic turn will not necessarily operate as a democratizing influence, and there will not be the projected spread of participation right across the community.

Ordinary people and the media

In its dealing with ordinary people's participation in the media, this book has concentrated on those modes of participation which have generated claims of citizen empowerment, of the development of new forms of consumer sovereignty, of the achievement of a new level of democratic enfranchisement, or of a celebration of the performing self. It has focused on developments which are relatively new, and in which the participation of ordinary people tends to involve some kind of reference to or representation of their everyday lives. I would acknowledge, though, that there are many more instances than I have dealt with where ordinary people, or aspects of their everyday lives, are transformed into media content: the rise of the TV makeover show, for instance, or the increasing number of lifestyle shows in which an ordinary person is put through some kind of encounter with an 'expert' who tells them how they can change their lives.

Nonetheless, in my opinion, the contradictions that are embedded in the media activities I have examined in this book can be found in these other locations and genres as well. On one hand, one can claim that the encounter with the expert should carry some personal benefits in terms of passing on useful advice that might otherwise not be available to that person. On the other hand, the authority of the 'expert' cannot be taken for granted in an entertainment-based genre, and the mere fact of the ordinary person's access to the media centre carries with it a level of public exposure that can itself generate other, and significant, risks. Yes, these formats do indeed provide new levels of access to ordinary people – in many instances, of a more diverse mix of 'race', ethnicity and class than before – but what is done with that access needs to be examined in relation to the specifics of the case. The makeover programme, for instance, has many formations. In virtually all of them, the subject of the makeover is not only open to but grateful for the opportunity; in *Extreme Makeover*, potential recipients of a makeover compete for the chance to be selected. Often, it is clear that the person concerned is well pleased with the results, for themselves and for those connected with them. And yet, even the most benign and least invasive of the makeover shows (*How to Look Good Naked*, or *Queer Eye for the Straight Guy*, or *You Are What You Eat*) commodifies the renovation of the person, demonstrating how their subject can respond to a more informed strategy of consumption. The more invasive ones certainly go further, medicalizing the dissatisfaction with one's physical appearance as a condition that requires surgical intervention. Overall, these shows participate, in one way or another, in a pathologization of either the body or the performance of the self.

Of course, at the most extreme ends of demotic media participation, we have ordinary people uploading naked images of themselves or webcam videos where they perform sexually as a means of attracting a following on the internet. Or, we have extravaganzas of exploitation such as the television game show format, *Moment of Truth*, which exposes contestants to a lie detector's assessment of their answers to questions provided by friends and family aimed at revealing serious and longstanding secrets, indiscretions or betrayals – all in front of a live audience. Notwithstanding the production team's assurances of counsellors waiting offstage, it is hard to see whether the personal price likely to be paid for this kind of participation is worth it (or the million-dollar prize, for that matter), and yet there seems to be no shortage of contestants.[2] And for those who seek access to the media for professional ends – as a means of kick-starting a career or developing publicity for a personal profile – the outcomes are not at all guaranteed. Indeed, in the midst of the demotic turn, the standard arrangements for the media economy haven't really changed that much; even in the digital domain, ordinary people remain commodities to be exploited for the commercial gain of someone else. This happens at all levels of the enterprise:

> For most users the Internet is not free; they pay considerable money for hardware and cables, external drives, connectivity, software and upgrades, design features, and subscriptions. Content producers pay to have their work shown. The techno-libertarian model of the 1990s remains prevalent, which says that those who write software and provide the telco-infra-structure will make the money on the basis of the ignorant masses who are all too happy to hand over their content for free. How content producers are going to make a living is perceived as a personal problem that is rarely discussed. Most of them are amateurs and the few professionals generate their income through old media such as the printing press, film, television and radio. (Lovink, 2008: xxv)

In accounting for what has been gained and what has been lost as a result of this new pattern of incorporating ordinary people into the media, it seems to me that there is no overall profit and loss sheet that can cover each and every case. There are costs and there are benefits, but, in my view, there is little in the shifts in the current formats, platforms or behaviour of the media to encourage a view that something fundamental has happened which comprehensively rearranges the power relations currently framing the interaction between an ordinary person and the media. What has happened is significant, no doubt, and the range of some possibilities has increased as a result, but the outcomes are still more likely to be those which support the commercial survival of the major media corporations rather than those which support the individual or community interests of an ordinary citizen.

Finally, it is worth returning, then, to the paradox at the heart of the media's relation with ordinary people today. At the same time as we are hearing, often and from many different sources, that today's audience is making use of the media on their own terms, more than ever before, the ways in which the media might be seen to be explicitly meeting their obligations to the community, or making a contribution towards something like the public good, have in my view diminished. Or, as Natalie Fenton has framed it, the 'discourses of citizenship and participation have increased as they have become less and less practiced':

> Being political and enacting citizenship have become assimilated into and absorbed by the modes and contents of entertainment – personalization, dramatization, simplification, and polarization, a potentially antipolitical civic privatism of individuals ... (2009: 56)

On balance, the turn towards entertainment may prove to have constituted an impoverishment of the social, political and cultural function of the media; the replacement of something that was primarily information – as in, say, current affairs radio – with something that is primarily entertainment – as in, say, talk radio – is more realistically seen as generating a democratic deficit than a democratic benefit. Not everyone with an interest in this situation would take that view – hence the need to write a book such as this. For my part, it is hard not to regard the volume of those voices which have welcomed the enhanced role of the ordinary person in the media as effectively serving to drown out the sounds of those who might complain about the downgrading of other, perhaps more effective, measures through which the media made a positive contribution to everyday life.

Notes

1 Elsewhere I have published a discussion of what we might make of the Michael Moore phenomenon which considers these issues in more detail (Turner, 2005: 88–92).
2 Or viewers, for that matter. It was the one big hit of the beginning of the US 2008 television season, which coincided with the tail-end of the writer's strike.

Bibliography

Abu-Lughod, L. (2005) *Dramas of Nationhood: The Politics of Television in Egypt*. Chicago: University of Chicago Press.

Anderson, C. (2006) *The Long Tail: Why the Future of Business is Selling Less of More*. London: Hyperion.

Andrejevic, M. (2004) *Reality TV: The Work of Being Watched*. Lanham, MD: Rowman & Littlefield.

Andrejevic, M. (2007) *iSpy: Surveillance and Power in the Interactive Era*. Lawrence: University Press of Kansas.

Andrejevic, M. (2008) 'Watching television without pity: the productivity of online fans', *Television and New Media*, 9(1) January: 24–46.

Athique, A.M. (2009) 'From monopoly to polyphony: India in the era of television', in G. Turner and J. Tay (eds), *Television Studies after TV: Understanding Television in the Post-Broadcast Era*. London: Routledge. pp. 160–7.

Australian Communications and Media Authority (ACMA) (2007) Report No. 1485, *Breakfast with Alan Jones*, broadcast by 2GB on 5, 6, 7, 8, and 9 December 2005. Available at www.acma.gov.au

Bahnisch, M. (2009) 'The stuff that myths are made of', *Inside Story: Current Affairs and Culture*, 14 January. Available at http://inside.org.au/the-stuff- that-myths-are-made-of/ (last accessed 14 January 2009).

Bauder, D. (2008) 'Study of "Daily Show": it's a lot like O'Reilly', *Yahoo! News*, 8 May. Available at http://news.yahoo.com/s/ap/20080508/ap_en_tv/tv_daily_show (last accessed 12 May 2008).

Bazelgette, P. (2005) *Billion Dollar Game: How Three Men Risked it all and Changed the Face of Television*. London: TimeWarner Books.

Bennett, T., Savage, M., Silva, E., Warde, A., Gayo-Cal, M. and Wright, D. (2009) *Culture, Class, Distinction*. London: Routledge.

Biltereyst, D. (2005) 'Reality TV, troublesome pictures and panics: reappraising the public controversy around reality TV in Europe', in S. Holmes and D. Jermyn (eds), *Understanding Reality TV*. London: Routledge. pp. 91–110.

Biressi, A. and Nunn, H. (eds) (2008) *The Tabloid Culture Reader*. Maidenhead: McGraw-Hill and the Open University Press.

Bodey, M. (2007) 'Four decades of "God's great equaliser"', *The Australian*, 19 April, p. 15.

Bodey, M. and Karvelas, P. (2007) 'Guilty Jones attacks media watchdog', *The Australian*, 12 April, pp. 1–2.

Bonner, F. (2003) *Ordinary Television: Analyzing Popular TV*. London: SAGE.

Bottoms, R. (1995) 'Liddy's lethal advice: red meat for Republican voters?', *Fairness and Accuracy in Reporting, Extra*, July/August. Available at http://www.fair.org/index.php? page=1313 (last accessed 26 November 2008).

Brabazon, T. (2008) *Thinking Popular Culture: War, Terrorism and Writing*. London: Ashgate.

Bromley, M. (ed.) (2001) *No News is Bad News: Radio, Television and the Public*. London: Longman.

Bruns, A. (2008a) *Blogs, Wikipedia, Second Life, and Beyond: From Production to Produsage*. New York: Peter Lang.

Bruns, A. (2008b) 'Reconfiguring television for a networked, produsage context', *Media International Australia*, 126: 82–94.

Brunsdon, C. (2009) 'Television criticism and the transformation of the archive', *Television and New Media*, 10(1): 28–30.

Burgess, J. (2008) 'All your chocolate rain are belong to us?', in G. Lovink and S. Niederer (eds), *Video Vortex Reader: Responses to YouTube*. Amsterdam: Institute of Network Cultures. pp. 101–10.

Burgess, J. and Green, J. (2009) *YouTube: Online Video and Participatory Culture*. Cambridge: Polity.

Calhoun, C. (2007) *Nations Matter: Culture, History and the Cosmopolitan Dream*. London: Routledge.

Castells, M. (2000) *The Rise of the Network Society* (2nd edn). Oxford and Malden, MA: Blackwell.

Chua, B.-H. (ed.) (2000) *Consumption in Asia*. London and New York: Routledge.

Collins, S. (2008) 'Making the most out of 15 minutes: reality TV's dispensable celebrity', *Television and New Media*, 9(2): 87–110.

Conboy, M. (2008) 'Foreword', in A. Biressi and H. Nunn (eds), *The Tabloid Culture Reader*. Maidenhead: McGraw-Hill and the Open University Press. pp. xv–xvi.

Couldry, N. (2003) *Media Rituals: A Critical Approach*. London: Routledge.

Couldry, N. (2004) 'Media meta-capital: extending the range of Bourdieu's field theory', *Theory and Society*, 32(5/6): 653–77.

Couldry, N., Livingstone, S. and Markham, T. (2007) *Media Consumption and Public Connection: Beyond the Presumption of Attention*. London: Palgrave Macmillan.

Couldry, N. and Markham, T. (2007) 'Celebrity culture and public connection: bridge or chasm?', *International Journal of Cultural Studies*, 10(4): 403–22.

Crofts, S. and Turner, G. (2007) 'Jonestalk: the specificity of Alan Jones', *Media International Australia*, 122: 132–49.

Curran, J. and Park, M.-J. (eds) (2004) *DeWesternizing Media Studies*. London: Routledge.

Davis, R. (2008) 'A symbiotic relationship between journalists and bloggers', Joan Shorenstein Center on the Press, Politics and Public Policy, Discussion Paper Series, John F. Kennedy School of Government, Harvard University.

Deggans, E. (2008) 'Old school TV news rules vs the new school', *The Feed*. Available at http://blogs.tampabay.com/media/2008/05/old-scholl-tv-n.html (last accessed 20 May 2008).

Deloitte (2009) 'State of the media democracy 2009 survey', 7 January. Available at http://www.deloitte.com/us/realitycheck (last accessed 30 January 2009).

Dovey, J. (2000) *Freakshow: First Person Media and Factual Television*. London: Pluto.

Ellis, J. (2002) *Seeing Things: Television in the Age of Uncertainty*. London and New York: Taurus.

eMarketer (2008) 'Blogs and traditional media: old media adds bit of the new', 22 May. Available at http://www.emarketer.com/Articles/Print.aspx?id=1006327&src=print_article_blue_b (last accessed 27 May 2008).

Este, J., Warren, C., Connor, L., Brown, M., Pollard, R. and O'Connor, T. (2008) *Life in the Clickstream: The Future of Journalism*. Sydney: Media Arts and Entertainment Alliance and the Walkley Foundation.

Fenton, N. (2009) 'My media studies: getting political in a global, digital age', *Television and New Media*, 10(1): 55–7.

Flew, T. and Wilson, J. (forthcoming) 'Journalism as social networking: the Australian youdecide project and the 2007 federal election', *Journalism: Theory, Practice and Criticism*.

Flint, D. (2007) 'Inquisitors curtailing freedom of speech', *The Australian*, 13 April, p. 14.

Franklin, B. (1997) *Newszak and News Media*. London: Edward Arnold.

Frith, S. (1991) 'The good, the bad, and the indifferent: defending popular culture from the populists', *Diacritics*, 21(4): 101–15.

Fung, A. (2008) *Global Capital, Local Culture: Transnational Media in China*. New York: Peter Lang.

Fung, A. (2009) 'Globalized television culture: the case of China', in G. Turner and J. Tay (eds), *Television Studies after TV: Understanding Post-Broadcast Television*. London: Routledge. pp. 178–88.

Gauntlett, D. (2007) 'Media Studies 2.0', *Theory.org*, 24 February. Available at http://www.theory.org.uk/mediastudies2-print.htm (last accessed 16 December 2008).

Glasser, T.L. (ed.) (1999) *The Idea of Public Journalism*. New York: Guilford.

Goggin, G. and Hjorth, L. (eds) (2008) *Mobile Technologies*. London and New York: Routledge.

Goggin, G. and McLelland, M. (eds) (2009) *Internationalising Internet Studies: Beyond Anglophone Paradigms*. London: Routledge.

Goot, M. (2008) 'Is the news on the Internet different? Leaders, frontbenchers and other candidates in the 2007 Australian election', *Australian Journal of Political Science*, 43(1): 99–110.

Gould, L. (2007) 'Cash and controversy: a short history of commercial talkback radio', *Media International Australia*, 122: 81–95.

Gregg, M. (2008) 'The normalisation of flexible female labour in the information economy', *Feminist Media Studies*, 8(3): 285–99.

Guido Fawkes Blog (2008) 'About Guido's blog'. Available at www.order-order.com.2004/01/about-guidos-blog.html (last accessed 11 December 2008).

Guthrie, M. (2008) 'Lack of foreign resources plagued U.S. Mumbai coverage', *Broadcasting & Cable*, 3 December. Available at http://www.broadcastingcable.com/CA6619222.html (last accessed 5 December 2008).

Hage, G. (2003) *Against Paranoid Nationalism: Searching for Hope in a Shrinking Society*. Sydney: Pluto.

Hallin, D. (1994) *We Keep America on Top of the World: Television Journalism and the Public Sphere*. London and New York: Routledge.

Hamm, T. (2008) *The New Blue Media: How Michael Moore, MoveOn.org, Jon Stewart and Company are Transforming Progressive Politics*. New York and London: The New Press.

Harris, J.F. (2008) 'How small stories become big news', *Politico*, 27 May. Available at http://dyn.politico.com/printstory.cfm?uuid+203F9A7D-3048-5C12-00F893045DC51 (last accessed 29 May 2008).

Hartley, J. (1996) *Popular Reality: Journalism, Modernity, Popular Culture*. London: Edward Arnold.

Hartley, J. (1999) *Uses of Television*. London: Routledge.

Hartley, J. (2008) *Television Truths*. Malden, MA: Blackwell.

Hartley, J. (2009) 'TV stories: from representation to productivity', in J. Hartley and K. McWilliam (eds), *Story Circle: Digital Storytelling Around the World*. Malden, MA: Wiley-Blackwell. pp. 16–36.

Hartley, J. and McWilliam, K. (eds) (2009a) *Story Circle: Digital Storytelling Around the World*. Malden, MA: Wiley-Blackwell.

Hartley, J. and McWilliam, K. (2009b) 'Computational power meets human contact', in J. Hartley and K. McWilliam (eds), *Story Circle: Digital Storytelling Around the World*. Malden, MA: Wiley-Blackwell. pp. 3–15.

Hay, J. and Ouellette, L. (2008) *Better Living Through Reality TV: Television and Post-Welfare Citizenship*. Malden, MA: Blackwell.

Hermann, E. and McChesney, R. (2001) *Global Media: The New Missionaries of Global Capitalism*. London: Continuum.

Hibbard, M., Kilborn, R., McNair, B., Marriott, S. and Schlesinger, P. (2000) *Consenting Adults?* London: Broadcasting Standards Commission.

Hill, A. (2008) *Restyling Factual TV: Audiences and News, Documentary and Reality Genres*. London: Routledge.

Hindman, M. (2007) 'Web traffic: the big picture'. Available at http://www.matthewhindman.com (last accessed 31 March 2008).

Hindman, M. (2008) 'I hate the bloggers', 8 July. Available at http://www.matthewhindman.com/index.php/2008070737/The-Myth-of-Digital-Democracy/-I-Hate-the-Bloggers.html (last accessed 11 December 2008).

Hindman, M. (2009) *The Myth of Digital Democracy*. Princeton and Oxford: Princeton University Press.

Hjorth, L. (2008a) 'Gifts of presence: a case study of a South Korean virtual community, Cyworld's mini-hompy', in G. Goggin and M. McLelland (eds), *Internationalising Internet Studies: Beyond Anglophone Paradigms*. London: Routledge. pp. 237–51.

Hjorth, L. (2008b) *Mobile Media in the Asia Pacific: Gender and the Art of Being Mobile*. London: Routledge.

Hjorth, L. (2009) *Gaming Cultures and Place in the Asia-Pacific*. London: Routledge.

Hoggart, R. (1958) *The Uses of Literacy*. Harmondsworth: Penguin.

Holmes, S. (2005) '"All you've got to worry about is the task, having a cup of tea, and doing a bit of sunbathing": approaching celebrity in *Big Brother*', in S. Holmes and D. Jermyn (eds), *Understanding Reality Television*. London: Routledge. pp. 111–35.

Holmes, S. and Jermyn, D. (eds) (2005) *Understanding Reality TV*. London: Routledge.

Jarrett, K. (2008a) 'Beyond broadcast yourself: the future of YouTube', *Media International Australia*, 126, February: 132–44.

Jarrett, K. (2008b) 'Interactivity is evil! A critical investigation of Web 2.0', *First Monday*, 13(3), March. Available at http://www.uic.edu/ htbin/cgi-wrap/bin/ojs/index/php/fm/article/view/2140/1947> (last accessed 10 April 2008).

Jenkins, H. (2006) *Convergence Culture: Where Old and New Media Collide*. New York: New York University Press.

Jenkins, H. (2008) 'Why academics should blog', 8 April, Confessions of an Aca-Fan. Available at http://henryjenkins.org/2008/04/why_academics_should_blog.html (last accessed 21 January 2009).

Johnson, R. (2000) *Cash for Comment: The Seduction of Journo Culture*. Sydney: Pluto Press.

Journalism.org (2008) 'Journalism, satire or just laughs? "The Daily Show with John Stewart" examined'. Available at http://www.journalism.org./print/10953 (last accessed 12 May 2008).

Kay, J., Zeigelmueller, G.W. and Minch, K.M. (1998) 'From Coughlin to contemporary talk radio: fallacies and propaganda in American populist radio', *Journal of Radio Studies*, 5(1): 9–21.

Keane, M., Fung, A.Y.H. and Moran, A. (2007) *New Television, Globalisation, and the East Asian Cultural Imagination*. Hong Kong: Hong Kong University Press.

Kilborn, R. (2003) *Staging the Real: Factual Programming in the Age of Big Brother*. Manchester: University of Manchester Press.

Kraidy, M. (2009) *Reality Television and Arab Politics: Contention in Public Life*. New York: Cambridge University Press.

LaFetra, B. (2008) 'Online reviews second only to word of mouth as purchase influencer in US', Rubicon Consulting White Paper, 23 October. Available at http://rubiconconsulting.com/insight/whitepapers/2008/10/online-reviews-second-only-to.html (last accessed 9 January 2009).

Langer, J. (1998) *Tabloid Television: Popular Journalism and the 'Other' News*. London: Routledge.

Lawsky, D. (2008) 'American youth trail in internet use: survey', *Reuters*, 24 November. Available at http://www.reuters.com/articlePrint?articleId=USTREA4ANOMR20081124 (last accessed 25 November 2008).

Learmonth, M. (2008) 'One-way media lost the election as cable, interactive dominated', *Advertising Age*, 10 November. Available at http://adage.com/print?article_id=132350 (last accessed 12 November 2008).

Le Bon, G. (1960 [1901]) *The Crowd: A Study of the Popular Mind*. New York: Viking.

Lee, F.L.F. (2007) 'Talk radio listening, opinion expression and political discussion in a democratizing society', *Asian Journal of Communication*, 17(1): 78–96.

Liddle, R. (2008) 'After Jade's cancer, what next? "I'm a tumour, get me out of here?" ', *The Spectator*, 23 August, p. 18.

Limbaugh, R. (2008) 'About the show', Rush Limbaugh.com.home. Available at http://www.rushlimbaugh.com/home/about_the_show. guest.html (last accessed 27 October 2008).

Lotz, A. (2007) *The Television will be Revolutionized*. New York and London: New York University Press.

Lovink, G. (2008) *Zero Comments: Blogging and Critical Internet Culture*. New York and London: Routledge.

Lovink, G. and Niederer, S. (eds) (2008) *Video Vortex Reader: Responses to YouTube*. Amsterdam: Institute of Network Cultures.

Lumby, C. (2003) 'Real appeal: the ethics of reality TV', in C. Lumby and E. Probyn (eds), *Remote Control: New Media, New Ethics*. Melbourne: Cambridge University Press. pp. 11–24.

Maliki, J. (2008) 'Cultural identity and cultural representation on reality TV: an analysis of *Akademi Fantasia*'. Unpublished MPhil thesis, University of Queensland, Australia.

Malkin, M. (2008) 'More about Mrs Blago', 10 December. Available at http://michellemalkin.com/2008/12/10/more-about-mrs-blago/ (last accessed 11 December 2008).

Manovich, L. (2008) 'The practice of everyday (media) life', in G. Lovink and S. Niederer (eds), *Video Vortex: Responses to YouTube*. Amsterdam: Institute of Network Cultures. pp. 33–44.

Marshall, P.D. (1997) *Celebrity and Power: Fame in Contemporary Culture*. Minneapolis: University of Minnesota Press.

Masters, C. (2006) *Jonestown: The Power and Myth of Alan Jones*. Sydney: Allen & Unwin.

Mattussek, M. (1995) 'Tuning in to hate', *World Press Review*, 42: 26–7.

McChesney, R.W. (2007) *Communication Revolution: Critical Junctures and the Future of Media*. London and New York: The New Press.

McClure, J. (2008) 'Middleberg/SNCR survey of journalists reveals generational gap', *New Communications Review*, 25 November. Available at http://www.newcommreview.com/?p=1368 (last accessed 25 November 2008).

McGuigan, J. (1992) *Cultural Populism*. London: Routledge.

McMillin, D.C. (2007) *International Media Studies*. Malden, MA: Blackwell.

McWilliam, K. (2009) 'The global diffusion of a community media practice: digital storytelling online', in J. Hartley and K. McWilliam (eds), *Story Circle: Digital Storytelling Around the World*. Malden, MA: Wiley-Blackwell. pp. 37–75.

Miller, T. (1997) 'Radio', in S. Cunningham and G. Turner (eds), *The Media in Australia: Industries, Texts, Audiences*. Sydney: Allen & Unwin.

Miller, T. (2008) *Makeover Nation: The United States of Reinvention*. Columbus: Ohio State University Press.

Miller, T. (2009) 'Approach with caution and proceed with care: campaigning for the US presidency "after TV"', in G. Turner and J. Tay (eds), *Television After TV: Understanding Television in the Post-Broadcast Era*. London and New York: Routledge. pp. 75–82.

Mishra, G. (2008) 'My interview with the BBC on the role of citizen journalism in the Mumbai terrorist attacks', *Gauvronomics Blog*, 3 December. Available at http://www.gauravonomics.com/blog/my-interview-with-bbc-on-the-role-of-citizen-journalism-in-the-mumbai-terrorist-attacks/ (last accessed 5 December 2008).

Moran, J. (2006) 'Milk bars, Starbucks and *The Uses of Literacy*', *Cultural Studies*, 20(6): 552–73.

Nielsen Company (2008) 'Nielsen's three screen report: television, internet and mobile usage in the US', May. Available at www.nielsen.com/pdf/3_Screen_Report_May08_FINAL.pdf (last accessed 30 July 2008).

Nielsen Wire (2008) 'Top online brands for streaming video September 2008', 27 October. Available at http://blog.nielsen.com/nielsenwire/tag/video-census/ (last accessed 8 January 2009).

Noriega, C.A. (2009) 'My media studies: straddling good fences', *Television and New Media*, 10(1): 119–21.

Nylund, D. (2004) 'When in Rome: heterosexism, homophobia and sports talk radio', *Journal of Sport and Social Issues*, 28(2): 136–68.

Ofcom (Office of Communications, UK) (2007) 'New news, future news: the challenges for television news after digital switchover', London, June. Available at http://www.ofcom. org.uk/research/tv/reports/newnews/ newnews. pdf (last accessed 26 November 2008).

Pesce, M. (2006) '"Hypercasting" hyperpeople: what happens after we're all connected?', 16 October. Available at http://blog. futurestreet consulting.com/?p=20 (last accessed 17 December 2008).

Pew Research Center for the People and the Press (2008) 'Key news audiences now blend online and traditional sources: audience segments in a changing environment', 17 August. Available at http://pewresearch.org/pubs/928/key-news-audiences-now-blend-online-and-traditional-sources (last accessed 12 September 2008).

Probyn, E. (2005) *Blush: Faces of Shame*. Sydney: University of New South Wales Press.

Project for Excellence in Journalism (2008) *The State of the News Media: An Annual Report on American Journalism*. Available at http//: www.stateofthenewsmedia.org/2008/ (last accessed 31 March 2008).

Rahman, M. (2008) 'Jade's confession: racism and the dialectics of celebrity', *Social Semiotics*, 18(2): 133–48.

Rojek, C. (2001) *Celebrity*. London: Reaktion.

Roscoe, J. (2001a) '*Big Brother* Australia: performing the real twenty-four seven', *International Journal of Cultural Studies*, 4(4): 473–88.

Roscoe, J. (2001b) 'Real entertainment: real factual hybrid television', *Media International Australia*, 100: 9–20.

Rosen, J. (2006) 'The people formerly known as the audience', *PressThink: Ghost of Democracy in the Media Machine*, 27 June. Available at http://journalism.nyu.ed/pubzone/weblogs/pressthink/2006/06/27/ppl_frmr.html (last accessed 25 November 2008).

Ross, A. (1989) *No Respect: Intellectuals and Popular Culture*. New York: Routledge.

Ross, A. (2004) *No Collar: The Humane Workplace and its Hidden Costs*. Philadelphia: Temple University Press.

Ross, A. (2009) 'The political economy of amateurism', *Television and New Media*, 10(1): 136–7.

Ross, K. (2004) 'Political talk radio and democratic participation: caller perspectives on *Election Call*', *Media, Culture and Society*, 26(6): 785–801.

Schiffman, B. (2008) ' "Citizen journalist" could face prison for fake jobs story', *Wired: Blog Network*, 3 October. Available at http://blog.wired.com/business/2008/10/cnn-citizen-jou.html (last accessed 8 October 2008).

Sconce, J. (2000) *Haunted Media: Electronic Presence from Telegraphy to Television*. Durham, NC, and London: Duke University Press.

Shanahan, M. (2007) 'Making waves: controversial celebrity newsman Geraldo Rivera is no stranger to rough weather, on land or on sea', *Boston Globe*, 1 September. Available at http://www.boston.com/news/globe/living/articles/2007/09/01/making_waves/ (last accessed 12 December 2008).

Shattuc, J. (1998) 'Go Ricki: politics, perversion and pleasure in the 1990s', in C. Geraghty and D. Lusted (eds), *The Television Studies Book*. London: Edward Arnold.

Shirky, C. (2008) *Here Comes Everybody: The Power of Organizing without Organizations*. New York: Penguin.

Skeggs, B. (2005) 'The making of class and gender through visualizing moral subject formations', *Sociology*, 39(5): 965–82.

Skeggs, B., Thumim, N. and Wood, H. (2008) 'Oh goodness, I am watching reality TV: how methods make class in audience research', *European Journal of Cultural Studies*, 11(5): 5–24.

Strike Force Neil (2006) *Cronulla Riots: Review of the Police Response*, Vol. 1. Sydney: NSW Police.

Sun, W. and Zhao, Y. (2009) 'Television culture with "Chinese characteristics": the politics of compassion and education', in G. Turner and J. Tay (eds), *Television Studies after TV: Understanding Post-Broadcast Television*. London and New York: Routledge. pp. 96–104.

Tacchi, J. (2009) 'Finding a voice: participatory development in Southeast Asia', in J. Hartley and K. McWilliam (eds), *Story Circle: Digital Storytelling Around the World*. Malden, MA: Wiley-Blackwell. pp. 167–75.

Tapscott, D. and Williams, A.D. (2006) *Wikinomics: How Mass Collaboration Changes Everything*. London: Portfolio.

Tebbutt, J. (2002) 'Hosting politics: disaffection and the genealogy of talkback'. Unpublished paper, Australian and New Zealand Communications Association conference, Coolangatta, Queensland, Australia.

Technorati (2008) 'State of the blogosphere 2008', 26 November. Available at http://technorati.com/blogging/state-of-the-blogosphere/ (last accessed 27 November 2008).

Terranova, T. (2000) 'Free labor: producing culture for the digital economy', *Social Text*, 18(2): 33–58.

Thissu, D. (2009) *Internationalising Media Studies: Impediments and Imperatives*. London: Routledge.

Turner, G. (1999) 'Tabloidization, journalism and the possibility of critique', *International Journal of Cultural Studies*, 2(1): 59–76.

Turner, G. (2003) 'Ethics, entertainment and the tabloid: the case of talkback radio', in C. Lumby and E. Probyn (eds), *Remote Control: New Media, New Ethics*. Melbourne: Cambridge University Press. pp. 87–99.

Turner, G. (2004) *Understanding Celebrity*. London: SAGE.

Turner, G. (2005) *Ending the Affair: The Decline of Television Current Affairs in Australia*. Sydney: University of New South Wales Press.

Turner, G. (2006) 'The mass production of celebrity: celetoids, reality TV and the "demotic turn"', *International Journal of Cultural Studies*, 9(2): 153–66.

Turner, G. (2007) 'Some things we should know about talkback radio', *Media International Australia*, 122: 73–80.

Turner, G. (2009a) 'Politics, radio and journalism in Australia: the influence of talkback', *Journalism: Theory, Practice and Criticism*, 10(4): 411–30.

Turner, G. (2009b) 'Television and the nation: Does this matter any more?' in G. Turner and J. Tay (eds), *Television Studies after TV*. London and New York: Routledge. pp. 54–64.

Turner, G., Bonner, F. and Marshall, P.D. (2000) *Fame Games: The Production of Celebrity in Australia*. Melbourne: Cambridge University Press.

Turner, G. and Tay, J. (eds) (2009) *Television Studies after TV: Understanding Post-Broadcast Television*. London and New York: Routledge.

Turner, G., Tomlinson, E. and Pearce, S. (2006) 'Talkback radio: some notes on format, politics and influence', *Media International Australia*, 118: 107–19.

Volcic, Z. (2007) 'Yugo-nostalgia: cultural memory and media in the former Yugoslavia', *Critical Studies in Mass Communication*, 1(24): 21–38.

Volcic, Z. (2009) 'Television in the Balkans: commercial nationalism', in G. Turner and J. Tay (eds), *Television Studies after TV: Understanding Television in the Post-Broadcast Era*. London and New York: Routledge. pp. 115–24.

Whenman, G. (2008) 'The top UK political blogs', *Total Politics*, 4 September. Available at http://www.totalpolitics.com/blogs/campaignsblog.php/2008/09/04/the-top-100-uk-political-blogs (last accessed 12 December 2008).

Young, S. (forthcoming) 'The decline of traditional news and current affairs and the fragmentation of news audiences in Australia', *Media International Australia*, 131.

Yue, A. and Yu, H. (2008) 'China's super girl: mobile youth cultures and new sexualities', in U.M. Rodrigues and B. Smaill (eds), *Youth, Media and Culture in the Asia Pacific Region*. Newcastle: Cambridge Scholars. pp. 117–34.

Index

Supporting researchers for more than forty years

Research methods have always been at the core of SAGE's publishing. Sara Miller McCune founded SAGE in 1965 and soon after, she published SAGE's first methods book, *Public Policy Evaluation*. A few years later, she launched the Quantitative Applications in the Social Sciences series – affectionately known as the 'little green books'.

Always at the forefront of developing and supporting new approaches in methods, SAGE published early groundbreaking texts and journals in the fields of qualitative methods and evaluation.

Today, more than forty years and two million little green books later, SAGE continues to push the boundaries with a growing list of more than 1,200 research methods books, journals, and reference works across the social, behavioural, and health sciences.

From qualitative, quantitative and mixed methods to evaluation, SAGE is the essential resource for academics and practitioners looking for the latest in methods by leading scholars.

www.sagepublications.com